Key Stage 3 English Kit

Year 9

Chris Webster

Hodder & Stoughton
A MEMBER OF THE HODDER HEADLINE GROUP

Acknowledgements

The author and publishers would like to thank the following:

Copyright Text:
Sutton Hoo Ship Burial © David Ross, taken from www.britainexpress.com/History/sutton-hoo.htm; Rune Poem translation © Tom Wulf; *The Curse of the Play* © Robert Faires, originally published in The Austin Chronicle, Austin, TX USA; *Holinshed's Chronicles of Scotland* by Raphael Holinshed, AMS Press, 1997; *The Adventure of the Speckled Band* by Sir Arthur Conan Doyle; Martin Guerre Trials taken from *Courtroom Drama: 120 of the World's Most Notable Trials* by Elizabeth Frost-Knappman, Edward W Knappman and Lisa Paddock (eds), Gale Group; 'All that I Love' from *Martin Guerre – The Boublil and Schonberg Musical* 4th version; 'Rhapsody on a Windy Night' © T.S. Eliot, from *Collected Poems 1909–1962*, Faber & Faber Ltd; 'Bukit Timah, Singapore' by Lee Txu Pheng, from *The Seven Poets*, Singapore University Press (PTE) Ltd; 'Toads' by Philip Larkin, reprinted from *The Less Deceived* by permission of The Marvell Press, England and Australia; 'Follower' © Seamus Heaney, from *Death of a Naturalist*, Faber & Faber Ltd; 'The Future' © Roger McGough as printed in the original volume, reprinted by permission of PFD on behalf of Roger McGough; 'I Mediate', 'News at Ten', 'Superstar on Guitar' & 'Modern Slavery' from *The Dread Affair* © Benjamin Zephaniah, Arrow Books Ltd; *'Black English' proposal draws fire* taken from Cable News Network (www.cnn.com); 'Pen Rhythm' from *The Dread Affair* © Benjamin Zephaniah, Arrow Books Ltd.

Copyright Photograph:
Page 115, Cecil Spring-Rice © Hulton-Deutsch Collection/Corbis.

Every effort has been made to trace copyright holders of material reproduced in this book. Any rights not acknowledged here will be acknowledged in subsequent printings if notice is given to the publisher.

Visit www.english-kit-hodder.co.uk for more Key Stage 3 English Kit resources by Chris Webster.

Orders: please contact Bookpoint Ltd, 78 Milton Park, Abingdon, Oxon OX14 4TD. Telephone: (44) 012345 827720, Fax: (44) 01235 400454. Lines are open from 9.00am – 6.00pm, Monday to Saturday, with a 24-hour message answering service. Email address: orders@bookpoint.co.uk

British Library Cataloguing in Publication Data
A catalogue record for this title is available from The British Library

ISBN 0 340 79075 X

First published 2001
Impress number 10 9 8 7 6 5 4 3 2 1
Year   2007 2006 2005 2004 2003 2002 2001

Copyright © 2001 Chris Webster

Cover image by Mike Preston (The Organisation)
Typeset by Fakenham Photosetting Limited, Fakenham, Norfolk NR21 8NN.
Printed in Great Britain for Hodder & Stoughton Educational, a division of Hodder Headline Plc, 338 Euston Road, London NW1 3BH by Hobbs the Printers, Totton, Hampshire.

Contents

National Strategy Key Stage 3 English Framework Objectives mapped to The Key Stage 3 English Kit

WORD LEVEL

Objective	KS3 English Kit – Yr 9
Wd:	various: Unit 1 – Lesson 8 Unit 4 – Lesson 10 Unit 6 – Lesson 2; final lessons
6	Unit 1 – Lesson 1; 5 Unit 2 – Lesson 5 Unit 4 – Lesson 3; 4 Unit 5 – Lesson 8
7	Unit 1 – Lesson 3 Unit 2 – Lesson 2; 4 Unit 3 – Lesson 3; 4; 5 Unit 5 – Lesson 2; 4
8	Unit 5 – Lesson 3

SENTENCE LEVEL

Objective	KS3 English Kit – Yr 9
Sn:	various: Unit 1 – Lesson 8 Unit 4 – Lesson 10 Unit 6 – Lesson 2; final lessons
2	Unit 4 – Lesson 2
4	Unit 1 – Lesson 2 Unit 3 – Lesson 3
5	Unit 2 – Lesson 7
6	Unit 1 – Lesson 4; 7
7	Unit 3 – Lesson 4; 5; 6
10	Unit 3 – Lesson 8 Unit 5 – Lesson 5; 6 Unit 6 – Lesson 1
11	Unit 2 – Lesson 3; 4 Unit 3 – Lesson 7

TEXT LEVEL – READING

Objective	KS3 English Kit – Yr 9
Rd:	various Unit 6, final lessons
1	Unit 2 – Lesson 1
2	Unit 3 – Lesson 7
6	Unit 2 – Lesson 5; 7 Unit 3 – Lesson 6 Unit 4 – Lesson 7; 8
7	Unit 3 – Lesson 8
8	Unit 3 – Lesson 1; 2 Unit 4 – Lesson 9
9	Unit 4 – Lesson 2
11	Unit 1 – Lesson 8 Unit 6 – Lesson 4
12	Unit 2 – Lesson 4 Unit 3 – Lesson 5 Unit 4 – Lesson 1; 4 Unit 5 – Lesson 1
14	Unit 3 – Lesson 4 Unit 4 – Lesson 5; 6
15	Unit 3 – Lesson 3
16	Unit 1 – Lesson 1; 3; 5 Unit 2 – Lesson 2; 3; 8 Unit 5 – Lesson 4; 5; 6; 7; 8
17	Unit 5 – Lesson 3
18	Unit 2 – Lesson 6 Unit 4 – Lesson 3 Unit 5 – Lesson 2

TEXT LEVEL – WRITING

Objective	KS3 English Kit – Yr 9
Wr:	various: Unit 6, final lessons
4	Unit 1 – Lesson 8 Unit 2 – Lesson 1
5	Unit 1 – Lesson 1; 6; 7
8	Unit 2 – Lesson 4
9	Unit 2 – Lesson 3; 7 Unit 4 – Lesson 1 Unit 5 – Lesson 7 Unit 6 – Lesson 4
13	Unit 3 – Lesson 1; 2; 3; 4; 5 Unit 5 – Lesson 6
14	Unit 2 – Lesson 6 Unit 4 – Lesson 4
16	Unit 3 – Lesson 6; 7 Unit 4 – Lesson 7; 8; 9 Unit 6 – Lesson 2
17	Unit 4 – Lesson 3 Unit 5 – Lesson 1; 2; 3; 4; 8

SPEAKING AND LISTENING

Objective	KS3 English Kit – Yr 9
S&L:	various: Unit 6, final lessons
2	Unit 2 – Lesson 1
3	Unit 2 – Lesson 8
5	Unit 3 – Lesson 5
7	Unit 3 – Lesson 8
9	Unit 1 – Lesson 2; 4; 5; 6 Unit 2 – Lesson 6 Unit 3 – Lesson 6; 7 Unit 4 – Lesson 7; 10 Unit 5 – Lesson 2; 4; 5
10	Unit 5 – Lesson 1
11	Unit 6 – Lesson 1; 3
13	Unit 3 – Lesson 1; 2; 3; 4
15	Unit 4 – Lesson 5; 6 Unit 6 – Lesson 1; 2; 3; 4

National Curriculum Key Stage 3 English Objectives mapped to The Key Stage 3 English Kit

En1 Speaking and Listening

Objective	KS3 English Kit – Yr 9
En1:	
1a	Unit 2
3a	Unit 6
4c	Unit 3
6f	Unit 2
6e	Unit 3; Unit 5
11b	Unit 6
11c	Unit 6

En2 Reading

Objective	KS3 English Kit – Yr 9
En2:	
1h	Unit 1
2a	Unit 2
5c	Unit 3
8a i	Unit 3
8a iii	Unit 4
8a vi	Unit 5
8b	Unit 2; Unit 6
8c	Unit 1; Unit 4; Unit 5
9b	Unit 4
9c	Unit 4

En3 Writing

Objective	KS3 English Kit – Yr 9
En3:	
1	Unit 2; Unit 3; Unit 5; Unit 6
1a	Unit 1; Unit 4
2	Unit 6
2a	Unit 1
2c	Unit 1

Introduction

Approaches to English teaching vary greatly, but it is probably fair to say that in recent years, many English departments have given too much emphasis to what the NLS calls 'text-level' skills, and too little to word and sentence-level skills. The National Literacy Strategy in KS3 has been introduced to help to redress this balance. It does so in two ways: a framework of objectives for word, sentence and text-level skills, the latter subdivided into reading, writing, speaking and listening, and a lesson plan that provides a structure, different in detail, but similar in intent to the primary 'literacy hour'.

Lessons begin with a *word or sentence activity* which provides an opportunity to focus on a skill which will be used later in the lesson. The *introduction* is often based on the reading of a *shared text* (a shared text is a text which the class or a group reads and studies together) and the *development* is often supported by writing frames, formats, checklists and other materials. The *plenary* provides an opportunity to reinforce the key objectives of the lesson.

The KS3 English Kit is meant to be more than a catchy title as the book has been designed to be a flexible 'kit of parts'. Indeed, to be strictly accurate, it is only part of a kit. The other parts are any existing lesson plans which a department wishes to adapt, and any lesson ideas from other published resources. It is also a kit in another sense of the word. Many of the resources, particularly the skills resources, but also the templates, checklists and word banks, are reusable in other lessons. Finally, the very nature of English teaching, for example, the availability of sets of books, means that the teaching sequence will be different for every teacher in the department. However, though the sequence can easily be varied, it is recommended that the Radio Simulation (Unit 6, Weeks 3/4), remains in the summer term as it is intended to consolidate some of the work of previous units. Even more important, the highly structured lesson plans are replaced with a more open-ended approach – the 'crutches' of templates, word banks, and teacher-led lessons are replaced by a project-based approach.

The KS3 English Kit contains five types of resources:

1. Teachers' Notes
These follow the recommended planning format for the KS3 NLS and can thus be photocopied and used as English department plans. Similarly, the overview for the book can be used as the medium-term plan for the whole year. All that is needed is to supplement the plans with material from existing departmental plans or other teaching resources where desired.

2. Skills resources
Skills resource sheets begin with an explanation and examples and continue with a number of tasks to help students to practise the skill. They are not lesson specific, and can be re-used in other lessons, in different ways as appropriate.

Use the explanation and examples for quick oral revision or teaching of a skill, then move on quickly to the main focus of the lesson. Students who have difficulty applying the skill during the lesson could be asked to do one or more of the tasks either straight away, in another lesson, or for homework. For new skills, or the more difficult skills, students could work through all the tasks on the sheet during the first ten minutes of the lesson.

Create a bank of skills resources, e.g. in a clearly labelled filing cabinet, and encourage students to refer to it as necessary. Students can also be given a skills resource by the teacher at any time for further practice. Note that the bank of skills resources in this book offers a comprehensive range of skills for this year group, though it could usefully be supplemented by other materials – see http://pwp.ibl.bm/~cawebster/ for a range of skills resources which can be freely downloaded.

3. Texts
Many of the lessons in this book are based on short texts which are provided. This means that the number of additional books which a department will have to purchase is kept to a minimum.

4 Templates and writing frames
Templates give broad structures for paragraphing and/or layout. Writing frames are similar, but include suggestions for phraseology. Most templates and writing frames are lesson specific, though the formats can easily be adapted to other

lessons. Generally, they are intended as guides. The blank spaces on the templates and writing frames should be used to make notes at the planning stage. However, some weaker students may find it easier to write directly onto the templates. In order to provide enough space for this, the resources will need to be enlarged to A3 size (double the size of the original).

It is a good idea to adapt some of the templates and writing frames so that they are generic rather than specific to a particular lesson, and add them to the resource bank described earlier.

 ### 5. Other resources
Stimulus materials – these vary greatly from card games to texts for sequencing. It is well worth preparing the reusable stimulus materials in advance. For example, illustrations on card games could be coloured (perhaps by students) and the cards pasted onto cardboard and laminated. They then become a good quality reusable resource which will last for a few years.

Checklists, word lists etc. – these should also be made available in the resource bank described earlier.

Most units, though not all, are based on a literary text chosen to meet the breadth of study requirements of the National Curriculum. Several will already be on the shelves of many English department stockrooms, others are less common and will have to be ordered. Usually, four key lessons are based on the text, the other lessons in the unit developing the theme through other resources, e.g. poetry and non-fiction, most of which are provided as photocopiables. This means that if the main text is not available, another text can be used in its place. Note that the key lessons will usually need to be supplemented by students reading sections of the text at home and by some additional lessons in school, as it takes quite some time to read the whole of a shared text.

All units are designed for mixed-ability English classes. Specific suggestions for differentiating the lessons are given in the teachers' notes, but the following general suggestions apply in most situations:

- Students who have problems with the starter activity could be given the resource sheet so that they can practise the skill on another occasion or at home. Some starter activities are cumulative, e.g. different levels of punctuating dialogue or constructing sentences. Students who have not mastered an earlier stage could be given additional practice at that stage.

- After reading a text to a class, ask students, working in groups of 4–6, to re-read the text, taking turns reading aloud. This gives weaker readers additional practice in reading in a supportive context (as opposed to reading to the whole class).

- Support materials such as formats and writing frames can be used at three levels. The very weakest students may find it helpful to write directly onto an enlarged copy of the template. Average students should use the template or writing frame as a guide, but follow it fairly closely. Able students should use them as a general guide but be encouraged to build on the basic framework. Note that templates and writing frames can be simplified, or enhanced for students of different ability.

Year 9, of course, is the year in which the National KS3 Tests take place. Generally, students who receive good teaching of the National Curriculum for English (and the National Literacy Strategy which is based on it) will be well prepared for the tests. However, the following resources will be found helpful in providing more specific support:

- *KS3 Revise National Tests English*, Letts, ISBN 1857589122

- http://www.bbc.co.uk/education/ks3bitesize/

A Note on Internet Addresses:

Several websites have been suggested throughout the book. By its nature, the world wide web is constantly changing, and it may be that some websites are no longer available. Having said that, many of the recommended websites have been reliably used by the author for a number of years.   Chris Webster, 2000.

Visit www.english-kit-hodder.co.uk for more Key Stage 3 English Kit resources by Chris Webster.

UNIT 1: GLOBAL TALES

> **Title of unit:** GLOBAL TALES
>
> **Resources**
> **Book:** *Global Tales: Stories from many Cultures*, ed. Michael Marland, Longman, ISBN 0582 28929 7.

Year: 9	**Term:** 1, first half	**Duration:** 8 lessons	**Set:** All

NLS objectives		**NC objectives**
Crime and Punishment	Wd6, Rd16, Wr5	En2 1h) reflect on the writer's presentation of ideas and issues, the motivation and behaviour of characters, the development of plot and the overall impact of a text.
Story Kit: Character	Sn4, S&L9	
What do you do in Winter?	Wd7, Rd16	En2 8c) fiction ... by major writers from different cultures and traditions.
Story Kit: Setting	Sn6, S&L9	En3 1a) draw on their experience of good fiction ...
An Astrologer's Day	Wd6, Rd16, S&L9	
Story Kit: Plot	Wr5, S&L9	En3 2a) plan, draft, redraft and proofread their work.
Story Kit: Beginnings and Endings	Sn6, Wr5	En3 2c) analyse critically their own and others' writing.
Redrafting	Wd: various, Sn: various, Rd11, Wr4	

Teaching sequence	**Outcomes**
Week 1: Crime and Punishment Story Kit 1: Character	Write notes on the 'Character File' template. *Write a character description.
Week 2: What do you do in Winter? Story Kit 2: Setting	Write an analysis of the author's description. *Write a description of a setting as part of a story (i.e. using the past tense). Write plot analyses of stories (books, films, TV).
Week 3: An Astrologer's Day Story Kit 3: Plot	*Write a detailed version of the plot of their own stories.
Week 4: Story Kit 4: Beginnings and Endings Story Kit 5: Redrafting	Write first draft of story. *Write final draft of story.
	Assessment pieces

Note: *Global Tales* works well with the 'Story Kit' lessons because the stories have been chosen with a focus on character, setting etc. However, if *Global Tales* is not available, other collections of short stories can be used with the 'Story Kit' lessons in a similar way.

Crime and Punishment

Unit 1: Lesson 1

70 minutes approx.

Objectives

Word: Wd6 know and use the terms that are useful for analysing language.

Reading: Rd16 analyse ways in which different cultural contexts and traditions have influenced language and style.

Writing: Wr5 explore different ways of opening, structuring and ending narratives and experiment with narrative perspective.

Word/Sentence Activity:

Revise the terms *adjective* and *adverb* (and the related terms *noun* and *verb*) and discuss their importance in character description.

Introduction:

Shared reading of 'Crime and Punishment', pp. 16–25 of *Global Tales*.

Development:

Working in pairs, students do the following tasks:

- List examples of adjectives and adverbs which are used to describe character, e.g. a *wicked* smile on his lips; he had corrected this error *repeatedly*; the boy *obstinately* said, etc.

- Do all three activities on pages 140–5.

- Explore the different techniques the author uses to create the character of the teacher or the boy by drawing up a chart like the one below:

ACTION	DIALOGUE	DESCRIPTION	COMMENTARY
the boy blinked etc.	'twenty-four'	. . . a wicked smile on his lips.	the boy was . . . being contrary on purpose

Plenary:

Discuss the activities.

Homework:

Write notes on one of the main characters (the boy or the teacher) using resource 1, the 'Character file' template.

Follow-up:

There are two other stories in the 'Focus on Character' section of *Global Tales*. One or both of these could be studied in follow-up lessons, or set for homework.

1. Character File

FULL NAME AND AGE	
APPEARANCE	
PERSONALITY – GOOD POINTS	
PERSONALITY – BAD POINTS	
INTERESTS	
WHERE HE/SHE LIVES	
WHERE HE/SHE WORKS OR STUDIES	
FAMILY BACKGROUND	
BIOGRAPHY	

Story Kit: Characters

Unit 1: Lesson 2

70 minutes approx.

Objectives

Sentence: Sn4 integrate speech, reference and quotation effectively into what they write.

Writing: (not listed) reveal character through an effective mix of action, dialogue, description and commentary.

Speaking and Listening: S&L9 discuss and evaluate conflicting evidence to arrive at a considered viewpoint.

Word/Sentence Activity:

In a quick question-and-answer session, recap on the basics of speech punctuation and layout, then move on to resource 2, which gives advice on developing dialogue. Note that students who have not mastered the basics should do more work on punctuation and layout instead.

Introduction:

With reference to 'Crime and Punishment' (pp. 16–25 of *Global Tales*) discuss the importance of character in stories. Explain that good stories depend on realistic characters. The more realistic a character is the more the reader cares what happens to him or her, and every event in the plot has more force.

A good way to develop realistic characters is to develop them in more detail than is actually needed for the story. Give them a full background so that you get to know them almost like real people. Give out the character cards (resource 3).

Development:

In groups of 3–4, students discuss the characters on the character cards. What are they like? Do they know any people like them? Where do they work or study? Where do they live? Etc.

Each student chooses a character to develop in more detail. This is done by filling in resource 1, Character file. Encourage students to use their imagination to develop a complete background for the character. They may change the name of the character, but everything else they make up must fit the picture on the card.

Plenary:

Discuss the characters and how they have been developed.

Homework:

Students write a description of their character *as though it were part of a story*. To do this they will need to:

* Use the past tense.
* Select key details from those jotted down on resource 1.
* Express these in carefully structured sentences.

Follow-up:

Students, working in pairs, could randomly match pairs of characters, then write the conversations they might have, practising the skills on resource 2.

The character cards could be extended into a much more diverse resource by making additional cards. A good way to do this is to clip pictures out of magazines and paste them on cards of the same size. The whole set could be mounted on cardboard and laminated. It will then be an excellent reusable resource which will help students to develop characters in their writing.

2. Developing Dialogue

When you have mastered the basics of punctuating and setting out dialogue, you should try to make it sound interesting and true to life. Here are five foolproof steps to help you develop your dialogue.

1. USE A SYNONYM OF SAID

E.g.: answered, asked, begged, cried, explained, grumbled, joked, moaned, muttered, replied, screamed, shouted, sighed, snapped, whispered, yelled.

INSTEAD OF: 'I'm bored,' said Sarah.
YOU COULD WRITE: 'I'm bored,' sighed Sarah.

2. ADD AN ADVERB

E.g.: abruptly, angrily, bluntly, boastfully, calmly, courteously, crossly, enthusiastically, frankly, grumpily, hopefully, icily, loudly, merrily, miserably, moodily, nervously, politely, sadly, sarcastically, shyly, softly, sulkily, tactfully, timidly, unkindly.

INSTEAD OF: 'I'm bored,' said Sarah.
YOU COULD WRITE: 'I'm bored,' said Sarah sulkily.
OR: 'I'm bored,' sighed Sarah sulkily.

3. ADD A PHRASE OF DESCRIPTION

A participial phrase is particularly effective. Don't worry about the term, just add a comma followed by a phrase beginning with an -ing verb.

INSTEAD OF: 'I'm bored,' said Sarah.
YOU COULD WRITE: 'I'm bored,' said Sarah, throwing herself down on the settee.
OR: 'I'm bored,' sighed Sarah sulkily, throwing herself down on the settee.

4. FOR BEST RESULTS

Vary the way you write the reporting clause (the 'said' part of the sentence) from no reporting clause at all, to clauses with all the above techniques. Use your 'ear' to help you write what sounds best. When you read a story, take particular note of how the author handles dialogue.

5. HAVE A TRY!

Write a story with lots of dialogue – or revise an earlier one – and try out the above techniques.

3. Story Kit 1: Characters

JAKE

JENNA

JIM

JEAN

JOHN

JOAN

What Do You Do in Winter?

Unit 1: Lesson 3

70 minutes approx.

Objectives

Word: Wd7 recognise layers of meaning in the writer's choice of words.

Reading: Rd16 analyse ways in which different cultural contexts and traditions have influenced language and style e.g., *in a Welsh short story*.

Writing: (not listed) establish settings through an effective mix of action, dialogue, description and commentary.

Word/Sentence Activity:

Revise *personification*. Personification is a figure of speech in which human qualities are attributed to objects or ideas.

Introduction:

Shared reading of 'What do you do in Winter?', pp. 34–40 of *Global Tales*.

Development:

Working in pairs, students do the following tasks:

● Find examples of personification in the story.

● Do all three activities on pages 143–4.

● Highlight all the words and phrases that give a sense of place, e.g. 'small town', 'English strangers', etc.

● Explore the different techniques the author uses to create the setting by drawing up a chart like the one below:

ACTION	DIALOGUE	DESCRIPTION	COMMENTARY
the small town resolutely put on powder and lipstick . . . etc.	'It's very rude,' they said, 'to speak Welsh when you know we can't understand you.'	. . . the chapels tried to make themselves inconspicuous.	Welsh was its language all week.

Plenary:

Discuss the tasks.

Note: Personification is one of the main techniques used to describe the town, e.g.

DESCRIPTION	PERSONIFICATION, i.e. HUMAN QUALITY
the small town the chapels the town	resolutely put on powder and lipstick . . . tried to make themselves inconspicuous scrubbed off its make-up

Homework:

Using notes from the lesson, explain how the author created an effective sense of place in 'What do you do in Winter?'

Follow-up:

There are two other stories in the 'Focus on Setting' section of *Global Tales*. One or both of these could be studied in follow-up lessons, or set for homework.

Story Kit: Setting

Unit 1: Lesson 4

70 minutes approx.

Objectives

Sentence: Sn6 compare and use different ways of opening, developing, linking and completing paragraphs.

Writing: (not listed) establish settings through an effective mix of action, dialogue, description and commentary.

Speaking and Listening: S&L9 discuss and evaluate conflicting evidence to arrive at a considered viewpoint.

Word/Sentence Activity:

Investigate how paragraphs of description are organised, using resource 4 as a starting point.

Introduction:

Recap on how a sense of place was developed in 'What do you do in Winter?' (pp. 34–40 of *Global Tales*). Use this example to explain to students that realistic settings are important in bringing a story to life. A good way to develop a realistic setting is to describe it in more detail than is actually needed in the story so that it becomes real to the author. A good example of this is the author J. R. R. Tolkien who created the world of 'Middle Earth' for his stories. He drew a map of Middle Earth, invented several languages for the peoples of Middle Earth and even wrote the entire history of Middle Earth. Give out the settings cards (resource 5).

Development:

In groups of 3–4, students discuss the settings on the settings cards. What can they see? Where is it? What else can they imagine that is just outside the scene shown?

Each student chooses a setting to develop in more detail (in rough draft). The first thing they need to do is give a specific name to the place. The next step is to pick out carefully all the details in the picture. Finally, students should use their imagination to develop more of the world of which the picture is a part.

Plenary:

Discuss the settings and how they have been developed.

Homework:

Students write a description of their setting *as though it were part of a story*. To do this they will need to:

⬤ Use the past tense.

⬤ Select key details from the rough draft.

⬤ Express these in carefully structured sentences.

Follow-up:

Students, working in pairs, could randomly match characters and settings and imagine how the character might react in that setting. This could provide the basis of some story ideas.

The settings cards could be extended into a much more diverse resource by making additional cards. A good way to do this is to clip pictures out of magazines and paste them on cards of the same size. The whole set could be mounted on cardboard and laminated. It will then be an excellent reusable resource which will help students to develop settings in their writing.

4. Paragraph Organisation

Paragraphs of narration are usually organised *chronologically* (i.e. by *time*). However, paragraphs of description are often organised differently. Explanations of the main methods of *non-chronological* paragraph organisation are given below:

SPACE

The details of a scene are arranged in order of space. This method of organisation is used when it is important to the story that the reader understands where things are in relation to others.

IMPORTANCE

Details of a scene are described in order of importance. Usually the description builds from general and minor details up to the most important detail.

HUMAN VIEW

In this type of paragraph organisation, the details of the scene are described in order that the main character would notice them.

TASK 1:

Read these three paragraphs and state how each has been organised.

> The first thing Tom noticed was the old 'For Sale' sign near the gate of Hobbleton Hall. Somebody had scrawled across it 'Keep Out – Haunted'. Tom looked down the overgrown drive, and the house certainly looked haunted. The windows were black, frameless holes, and the roof was a skeleton of rotting timber . . .

> The castle keep was situated on a huge motte, one side of which descended into a steep valley. The other side, which was less steep, was defended by a massive curtain wall with round towers at regular intervals which provided platforms for cross-fire. In the centre of the wall was the gatehouse – definitely the castle's weakest point.

> Aliens of every shape and size crowded the spaceport departure lounge. Along both sides were shops selling souvenirs from all over the Kargish sector. Zena was particularly fascinated by the cyberpets – electronic simulations of pets that were not affected by quarantine regulations. At the end of the departure lounge was a huge plexi-glass window, and through it could be seen the rockets, each like a huge metal Empire-State building, pointing to the stars.

TASK 2:

Find examples of the different types of paragraph organisation in a story you are reading.

5. Story Kit 2: Setting

CITY CENTRE

OLD HOUSE

FOREST

AIRPORT

TROPICAL ISLAND

OUTDOOR MARKET

The Astrologer's Day

Unit 1: Lesson 5

70 minutes approx.

Objectives

Word: Wd6 know and use the terms that are useful for analysing language e.g. *relative pronouns*.

Reading: Rd16 analyse ways in which different cultural contexts and traditions have influenced language and style e.g., *in an Indian short story*.

Speaking and Listening: S&L9 discuss and evaluate conflicting evidence to arrive at a considered viewpoint.

Word/Sentence Activity:

Revise *relative pronouns* using resource 6, Relative Prounouns.

Introduction:

Shared reading of 'The Astrologer's Day', pp. 1–6 of *Global Tales*.

Development:

Ask students, working in pairs, to do the following activities:

- Find examples of relative pronouns and examine how they have been used to build up sentences.
- Carry out the activities on this story on p. 139 of *Global Tales*.

Plenary:

Discuss the activities.

Note:

The first two sentences of 'The Astrologer's Day' are both complex sentences which contain examples of relative pronouns. In the first sentence, the relative pronoun introduces a adjectival clause which describes the astrologer's equipment. The clause takes the form of a list. In the second sentence, the relative pronoun introduces an adjectival clause which describes the gleam in his eyes. To this a further clause is added (using the conjunction 'but') which qualifies the description of the gleam in his eyes.

Discuss the ending of the story. This kind of ending is called 'a twist in the tale', because it is an unexpected turn of events that brought his former enemy to seek his fortune, and at the same time made the astrologer seem uncharacteristically competent.

Homework:

Ask students to write plot analyses of any stories (from books, films or TV) that they know well. The next step is to discuss the plots and look for similarities.

Follow-up:

Read 'The Pieces of Silver', pp. 7–13 of *Global Tales*, and write a response to activity 3 on page 140.

6. Relative Pronouns

Relative pronouns are used to join statements together to create longer sentences. The commonest relative pronouns are *who, which* and *whose*.

EXAMPLE:

TWO STATEMENTS:

My father has a younger brother. The brother's name is James.

JOINED WITH THE RELATIVE PRONOUN 'WHOSE':

My father has a younger brother *whose* name is James.

Sometimes, the statements are joined by breaking one of the statements into two parts and placing the other inside it:

TWO STATEMENTS:

One of the lessons was about World War I. I found this the most interesting.

JOINED WITH THE RELATIVE PRONOUN 'WHICH':

One of the lessons, *which* I found the most interesting, was about World War I.

TASK 1:

Join these pairs of statements with an appropriate relative pronoun (*who, whose, which*). Break one of the statements if necessary.

The rabbit's only neighbour was a harmless old badger. The badger's earth was under the root of a tree.

Balloons are often filled with hydrogen. Hydrogen is the lightest gas.

Sir Walter Raleigh was executed by James I. He had been one of Queen Elizabeth's favourites.

Robert Stephenson designed the 'Rocket'. The 'Rocket' won the Rainhill trials.

TASK 2:

Find examples of relative pronouns in a text you are reading.

Story Kit: Plot

Unit 1: Lesson 6

70 minutes approx.

Objectives

Writing: Wr5 explore different ways of opening, structuring and ending narratives and experiment with narrative perspective.

Speaking and Listening: S&L9 discuss and evaluate conflicting evidence to arrive at a considered viewpoint.

Starter activity:

Demonstrate to students how to use one of the plot cards as a template for planning. This can be done by copying the outline plan on the card into the first column of a two-column planner (along with any modifications) and writing the specific story plan in the second column, e.g:

PLOT CARD – FLASHBACK	STORY PLAN – MISSION TO TITAN
The story begins with an exciting scene. A flashback then fills in the necessary background information. etc.	Description of the landing on Titan. Flashback describing the detailed preparation for the launch. etc.

Introduction:

Give out the Plot Cards (resource 7) and discuss the different types of plot.

Students (in groups of 4–5) to compare the cards with the plot analyses they did for homework. They should write on the back of each card the title of any story which has a similar plot.

The next step is to create new plot cards for any plot types that are not represented in the cards.

Development:

All three sets of cards are now brought together: Character, Setting and Plot. Students discuss their previous work on Character and Setting, and try to find a plot structure which will enable them to develop it into a story. If they wish, they can start again with a new character and setting.

Plenary:

Each group presents one example of a story based on the Character, Setting and Plot cards.

Homework:

Students write a detailed version of the plot of their story using the method described in the starter activity.

Follow-up:

Using the ideas from student discussion in the introductory session above, extend the range of plot cards for future use.

7. Story Kit 3: Plot

PROBLEM

Introduce the main character. Describe a problem that he/she has. Describe several attempts to solve the problem, each one more desperate than the other. The story ends when the problem is finally solved. An effective 'twist-in-the-tale' would be to make the solution something simple that the main character had overlooked.

QUEST

The main character has to search for something.
Describe the adventures the main character has during the search. Suspense can be developed by making the reader wonder: will he/she make it? In the end the main character finds what he/she is looking for – but was it what he/she expected?

SUBPLOT

A group of people is introduced. A problem or goal is described. The group splits into two. The hero's group tries to solve the problem or reach the goal one way, the other group in a different way. The narrative switches between one group and the other. The hero's group solve the problem or achieve the goal.

Y-PLOT

Character(s) and setting are introduced and a story starts to unfold. The narrative then switches to a completely different setting with different characters and story. The narrative switches back and forward as the two stories unfold. Eventually the two come together and it is suddenly clear how the two 'strands' of the story are linked. The plot then continues as one story until it reaches the end.

FLASHBACK

The story begins with an exciting scene. A flashback then fills in the necessary background information.
The story then continues (there may be other flashbacks). This is an effective technique which can easily be combined with other plot techniques.

WHODUNNIT

This is the classic crime fiction plot: a crime takes place. Certain characters are *suspects* because they have *motives*. *Clues* point to the villain, but a *red herring* is introduced. This is a character or event that distracts the reader from the real villain. At the end of the story the real villain is revealed and is punished.

Story Kit: Beginnings and Endings

Unit 1: Lesson 7

70 minutes approx.

> **Objectives**
>
> **Sentence:** Sn6 compare and use different ways of opening, developing, linking and completing pararaphs *and stories*.
>
> **Writing:** Wr5 explore different ways of opening, structuring and ending narratives and experiment with narrative perspective.

Word/Sentence Activity:

Discuss the different ways in which a paragraph can be opened, e.g. with a statement, a question, a participial phrase, an initial conjunction, an adverb, dialogue.

Introduction:

Shared reading of 'The Pieces of Silver', pp. 7–15 of *Global Tales*. Ask students to identify how each of the first six paragraphs are opened (use the list above as a guide).

Note:
Paragraph 1: initial conjunction
Paragraph 2: adverb
Paragraph 3: statement
Paragraph 4: statement
Paragraph 5: statement
Paragraph 6: initial conjunction

Development:

STAGE 1: Strange as it may seem, the first stage focuses on the Endings cards. The reason for this is that the ending of a story is the most difficult thing to get right, and any changes may affect the plot.

Give out the Endings cards (resource 8). These consist of examples of six types of story ending. An explanation of each type will be helpful:

◉ Happy-ever-after
The commonest type of ending in which everything works out OK.

◉ Anticlimax
Following a big build up of suspense, the story ends by revealing that it was all for nothing, e.g. a misunderstanding.

◉ Twist-in-the-tale
This type of ending reveals something which puts the events of the story in a different light. This is most effective in short stories where the beginning of the story is still fresh in the reader's mind.

◉ Circular
The main characters are back where they started, except that they have learned something or achieved something along the way.

◉ Cliff-hanger
This is an ending which leaves the reader in suspense about what happens. It is not a good way to end a story, but an excellent way to end a chapter, as it makes the reader want to read on.

● Proverb or moral
This is effective for stories of a specific type, such as fables. When writing this kind of ending it is a good idea to plan backwards from the ending so that everything in the story leads towards it.

Ask students to read all the endings and discuss which ones best suit their story idea and plot. They should adapt their plots if it helps to make an ending work better. The examples may give them some ideas about appropriate phraseology for their own ending.

Plenary 1:

Discuss students' ideas for ending their stories.

STAGE 2:
Once the plan has been refined to create an effective ending, the next step is to start writing. The beginnings of stories on the Beginnings Cards (resource 9) mainly focus on matters of style, and can be used as models for students to follow.

Give out the cards and ask students to read and discuss them in groups of 3–4.

Students then decide which type of beginning best suits their own story and make a start on writing.

Plenary 2:

Share some of the beginnings which students have written for their own stories.

Homework:

Begin the first draft of the final story.

Follow-up:

Discuss the first draft with other students.

8. Story Kit 4: Endings

HAPPY-EVER-AFTER

They were walking down the beach to the three rocks that stood in the sea. He watched them wade into the peacock blue and green sea, the foam breaking against their ankles, to scatter flower petals and coloured powder on the rocks as they prayed to the sea. He saw that his mother was amongst them.

'Lila, look!' he said. 'Look, Lila!'

The Village by the Sea by Anita Desai

ANTICLIMAX

Daylight at last! Tim screwed up his courage and went to investigate the wailing that had haunted him all night. It seemed to be coming from the next bedroom – there in the old wardrobe. Tim grasped the handle and pulled the door open suddenly, hardly daring to look – and there it was, the object of his terror – a little kitten.

North Hanger Abbey by J. A. Collins

TWIST-IN-THE-TALE

The dripping from the roof had turned into a trickle. I could see it coursing down the outside of the window; ice running free again. Tomorrow the downpour would crack and burst and gush back to life. But I would never see Rab again. I thought of him, a free spirit, urging the black horse on over the moors, riding free, laughing.

'I already knew that,' I said to her. 'Rab came back to tell me.'

Nightmare by Berlie Doherty

CIRCULAR

Sarah realised that she was back where she had started – in the bath, looking at her legs, wishing they weren't so hairy. She had been to hell and back, and still wasn't sure whether it had actually happened or whether it had been caused by the fever when she was ill. Still, at least she was sure about one thing – she was not a weregirl after all.

Weregirl by Amy Docherty

CLIFF-HANGER

Zarg pushed the button and the outer doors of the airlock swung open. Jeff found himself ejected into space as the remaining air gushed from the airlock. 'Hey!' he shouted, hoping that Zarg could hear him through the intercom, 'I'm really sorry that I joked about your sister! Let me back in.'

There was no reply. The only sound was the sound of his breathing – and there was only 30 minutes of air in the tank.

Aliens in Manchester by Dominic Parry

PROVERB OR MORAL

. . . when winter came, the Grasshopper found himself dying of hunger. He did not sing and dance then; he just lay still and watched the ants sharing out the food that they had collected in the summer.

Then the Grasshopper knew the truth of the old saying: 'It is wise to prepare for hard times.'

Aesop

9. Story Kit 5: Beginnings

DESCRIPTION OF A PLACE

When Lila went out on the beach it was so early in the morning that there was no one else there. The sand was washed clean by last night's tide and no one had walked on it except the birds that fished along the coast – gulls, curlews and sandpipers. She walked down to the sea with the small basket she carried on the flat of her hand, filled with flowers she had picked from the garden around their house.

The Village by the Sea by Anita Desai

DESCRIPTION OF A PERSON

Dr Rankin was a large and rawboned man on whom the newest suit at once appeared outdated, like a suit in a photograph of twenty years ago. This was due to the squareness and flatness of his torso, which might have been put together by a manufacturer of packing cases. His face also had a wooden and roughly constructed look; his hair was wiglike and resentful of the comb.

De Mortuis by John Collier

ACTION

When Eugene Ritter grasped the handle but was unable to open the door, he knew what had happened. His strength had not diminished, but no matter how hard he tried, he could not make the handle turn, or even rattle.

The Smile of Eugene Ritter by John Gordon

DIALOGUE

'There's someone coming down in the lift, Mummy!'

'No, my darling, you're wrong, there isn't.'

'But I can see him through the bars – a tall gentleman.'

'You think you can, but it's only a shadow. Now, you'll see, the lift's empty.'

And it always was.

Someone in the Lift by L. P. Hartley

FIRST PERSON

Never having tried keeping a diary before, it will be amusing to see whether I have enough mental energy to go on with it. At all events my new-found leisure will not give me the excuse of being too busy. The only question about it is – shall I find anything worth recording in this quiet, country existence?

The Meerschaum Pipe by L. A. Lewis

THIRD PERSON

Gran was not keen on Susan buying a car. She was inclined to be over-protective, and she thought Susan was much too young to be flying up and down motorways, especially late at night. But Susan was old enough – just – to get a licence, and by the time she'd passed her driving test she was old enough to spend the money too.

The Road Home by Jean Richardson

Redrafting

Unit 1: Lesson 8

70 minutes approx.

> ### Objectives
>
> **Word:** various
>
> **Sentence:** various
>
> **Reading:** Rd11 analyse how an author's standpoint can affect meaning in non-literary as well as literary texts.
>
> **Writing:** Wr4 choose, use and evaluate a range of presentational devices, on paper and on screen.

Word/Sentence Activity:

Revise the skills covered in this unit:

- adjectives and adverbs
- speech punctuation
- developing dialogue
- personification
- paragraph organisation
- relative pronouns
- planning
- paragraph openings

Allow students ten minutes to revise and practise any skill in which they are weak.

Introduction:

This lesson should take place when all students have finished the first draft of their story.

Give out resource 10, Story Kit 6: Redrafting, and explain it to students. The redrafting cards follow the format of the Story Kit. Each card contains prompt questions to help with the revision and development of the separate aspects of story writing covered by the kit. Note that the sheet of cards can be used as a whole, or cut up into separate cards to provide a focus on a particular aspect.

Development:

Students work in pairs as follows:

- One student reads his/her work to his/her partner.
- The partner highlights the areas on the cards which could be improved.
- Students discuss how to improve the highlighted areas.

Students then change roles and repeat the process.

Plenary:

Students share with the class how they improved their work through the redrafting process and read out examples of their stories 'before' and 'after' the process.

Homework:

Students complete work on redrafting and write out the final draft of their stories.

Follow-up:

The full six-card Story Kit can be used on future occasions as a support for story-writing.

10. Story Kit 6: Redrafting

CHARACTERS

Key Question:
Are the characters true to life?
You may be able to improve the characters by:

- adding more detail to their descriptions
- using more adjectives and adverbs
- using a few well-chosen figures of speech
- making them more real by referring more to their background
- developing the dialogue between characters

See Story kit 1

SETTINGS

Key Question:
Can the reader see the setting in his/her mind?
You may be able to improve the settings by:

- adding more detail to descriptions
- using more adjectives and adverbs
- using a few well-chosen figures of speech
- adding more, or more effective, telling details
- improving the organisation of descriptive paragraphs

See Story kit 2

PLOT

Key Questions:
Is it interesting?
Does it give a sense of going somewhere?
You may be able to improve the plot by:

- planning it more carefully
- adding a subplot
- adding a flashback
- adding more incidents
- building up suspense
- exploring your original story idea more fully

See Story kit 3

BEGINNING

Key Questions:
Does it grab the reader's attention?
Does it make the reader want to read on?
Are the beginnings of paragraphs varied in grammatical structure?

See Story kit 4

ENDING

Key Question:
Is the ending satisfying?
You may be able to improve the plot by:

- changing the type of ending used; or
- if a more effective type of ending cannot be found, thinking carefully about the wording of the ending you have – this can make a big difference.

See Story kit 5

PROOFREADING

Check:

- spelling
- punctuation
- grammar
- paragraphing

UNIT 2: BEOWULF

Title of unit: BEOWULF
Resources
Books: *Beowulf*, trans. by Seamus Heaney[1], ISBN 0571203760; *Grendel*, by John Gardner, ISBN 0860721418

Year: 9	Term: 1, second half	Duration: 8 lessons	Set: All

NLS objectives		**NC objectives**
Background	Rd1, Wr4, S&L2	En1 1a) structure their talk clearly, using markers so that their listeners can follow their line of thought.
Beowulf's Fight with Grendel	Wd7, Rd16	
The Haunted Mere	Sn11, Rd16, Wr9	En1 6f) the development of English, including changes over time.
Beowulf's Fight with The Dragon	Wd7, Sn11, Rd12, Wr8	En2 2a) how and why texts have been influential and significant.
The Monster's Point of View	Wd6, Rd6	En2 8b) recent and contemporary fiction.
Grendel Overview	Rd18, Wr14, S&L9	En3 1 Writing to inform, explain, describe; writing to analyse, review, comment.
Sutton Hoo	Sn5, Rd6, Wr9	
The Rune Poem	Rd16, S&L3	
Teaching sequence		**Outcomes**
Week 1: Background Beowulf's Fight with Grendel		Group presentation *Essay on the characters of Beowulf and Grendel
Week 2: The Haunted Mere Beowulf's Fight with The Dragon		Imaginative response to description of the mere. *Write an essay on the scene.
Week 3: The Monster's Point of View Grendel Overview		*Retell the story from another character's point of view *Write an essay on one of the characters.
Week 4: The Sutton Hoo Ship Burial The Rune Poem		*Write an essay linking Sutton Hoo to Beowulf. Write predictions from rune readings.
		*Assessment pieces

[1]NOTE: Seamus Heaney's award-winning translation is recommended as the basis for studying this poem. However, if this is not available, several versions are available on the world wide web. The 1910 Francis B. Gummere translation is available at:
http://rubens.anu.edu.au/raid1/student.projects/hoo2/beowulf1.html
This translation captures the flavour of the original language and the alliterative line, though it uses many archaic words and is difficult to follow in places.

Dr David Breedon's translation is available at: http://www.Instar.com/literature/beowulf/beowulf.html
This is a free verse translation in simple modern English. The story is divided into episodes, each with a helpful title, and is enlivened by illustrations.

Heaney's version combines the feel of the original language with a high level of readability.

The extracts referred to in the lesson plans are identified by line references to the original text and page references to Heaney's translation (paperback version) ISBN 0571 203760.

Background

Unit 2: Lesson 1

70 minutes approx.

Objectives

Reading: Rd1 review and extend their own strategies for locating, appraising and extracting relevant information.

Writing: Wr4 choose, use and evaluate a range of presentational devices, on paper and on screen.

Speaking and Listening: S&L2 use standard English to explain, explore or justify an idea.

Starter Activity:

In a brief discussion session, help students to review their research skills. Emphasise that the two most important skills are: the ability to use alphabetical order, and the ability to pick out key points.

Where appropriate, set follow-up tasks as necessary, e.g. on the Dewey decimal system.

LOCATING INFORMATION
- alphabetical order – contents and indexes
- Dewey decimal cataloguing
- skimming and scanning
- use of internet search engines

APPRAISING INFORMATION
- formulating research questions
- testing retrieved information against research questions
- appropriateness of retrieved information for purpose and audience

EXTRACTING INFORMATION
- note-making skills
- summary skills

Introduction:

Shared reading of resource 11, An introduction to *Beowulf*.

Development:

Further background research. This will depend on the resources available. Ideally, the lesson should take place in a library or computer room so that a wide range of books, or internet access is available.

The following questions can be used as a starting point. One way to organise the research is to give different groups of students different research questions.

- Who were the Anglo-Saxons?
- When did they come to Britain?
- Which countries did they come from?
- What were their religious beliefs (before Christianity)?
- What was their culture and way of life?
- What can you find out about their art, architecture, artefacts etc?

Useful web sites:

http://www.geocities.com/Athens/2471/main.html – 'Anglecynn' – an award-winning site with lots of useful information presented in an interesting way.

http://www.lauraloft.f2s.com/saxon/a-saxon.htm – this page contains a range of links to other sites about Anglo-Saxon England.

Plenary:

Students discuss what they have found out so far about the background to *Beowulf*.

Homework:

Each group prepares a presentation on its research question. This should include one page of key facts.

Follow-up:

The introduction to Heaney's translation is too academic for most students. However, it is well worth using parts of it to explain the relevance of *Beowulf* in today's world, e.g. p xxi where Heaney compares the keening of the Geat woman for her dead lord to the suffering of the victims in Rwanda.

11. An Introduction to *Beowulf*

Although the manuscript which contains the epic of Beowulf was written about AD 1000, the poem itself was known and had been elaborated upon for centuries by minstrels who recited the heroic exploits of the son of Ecgtheow and nephew of Hygelac, King of the Geats, whose kingdom was what is now Southern Sweden.

For twelve years, Hrothgar, King of Denmark, suffered while his kingdom was being ravaged by a devouring monster, named Grendel. This Grendel bore a charmed life against all weapons forged by man. He lived in the wastelands and nightly prowled out to visit the hall of Hrothgar, carrying off and slaughtering many of the guests.

Beowulf, hearing from mariners of Grendel's murderous visits, sailed from Geatland with fourteen stalwart companions to render Hrothgar the help of his great strength. Landing on the Danish coast, Beowulf was challenged as a spy. He persuaded the coastguards to let him pass, and he was received and feasted by King Hrothgar. When the king and his court retired for the night, Beowulf and his companions were left alone in the hall. All but Beowulf fell asleep. Grendel entered. With a stroke he killed one of Beowulf's sleeping men, but Beowulf, unarmed, wrestled with the monster and by dint of his great strength managed to tear Grendel's arm out at the shoulder. Grendel, mortally wounded, retreated, leaving a bloody trail from the hall to his lair.

All fear of another attack by Grendel allayed. the Danes returned to the hall, and Beowulf and his companions were sheltered elsewhere. Grendel's mother came to avenge the fatal injury to her monster son and carried off a Danish nobleman and Grendel's torn-off paw. Following the blood trail, Beowulf went forth to despatch the mother. Armed with his sword, Hrunting, he came to the water's edge. He plunged in and swam to a chamber under the sea. There he fought with Grendel's mother, killing her with an old sword he found in the sea cavern. Nearby was Grendel's body. Beowulf cut off its head and brought it back as a trophy to King Hrothgar. Great was the rejoicing in the hall and greater was Beowulf's welcome when he returned to Geatland, where he was given great estates and many high honors.

Shortly afterward, Heardred, the boy-king, was killed in the war with the Swedes. Beowulf succeeded him to the throne.

For fifty years Beowulf ruled his people in peace and serenity. Then suddenly a dragon, furious at having his treasure stolen from his hoard in a burial mound, began to ravage Beowulf's kingdom. Like Grendel, this monster left its den at night on its errand of murder and pillage.

Beowulf, now an aged monarch, resolved to do battle, unaided, with the dragon. He approached the entrance to its den, whence boiling steam issued forth. Undaunted, Beowulf strode forward shouting his defiance. The dragon came out, sputtering flames from its mouth. The monster rushed upon Beowulf with all its fury and almost crushed him in its first charge. So fearful grew the struggle that all but one of Beowulf's men deserted and fled for their lives. Wiglaf remained to help his aged monarch. Another rush of the dragon shattered Beowulf's sword and the monster's fangs sunk into Beowulf's neck. Wiglaf, rushing into the struggle, helped the dying Beowulf to kill the dragon.

Before his death, Beowulf named Wiglaf his successor to the throne of Geatland and ordered that his own ashes be placed in a memorial shrine at the top of a high cliff commanding the sea. Beowulf's body was burned on a vast funeral pyre, while twelve Geats rode around the mound singing their sorrow and their praise for the good and great man, Beowulf.

From THE AGE OF FABLE by Thomas Bulfinch, 1855

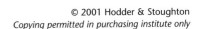

Beowulf's Fight with Grendel

Unit 2: Lesson 2

70 minutes approx.

> ### Objectives
>
> **Word:** Wd7 recognise layers of meaning in the writer's choice of words, e.g., *the use of hyperbole and litotes.*
>
> **Reading:** Rd16 analyse ways in which different cultural contexts and traditions have influenced language and style, e.g., *Anglo-Saxon heroic poetry.*

Word/Sentence Activity:

Define the following terms, particularly as they apply in Anglo-Saxon heroic poetry: *boasting, hyperbole* and *litotes*

Boasting:
In Anglo-Saxon heroic culture, boasts are admired – as long as the boaster lives up to them. However, nothing is more despised than an empty boast.

Hyperbole is a figure of speech which uses exaggeration for effect. In heroic poetry the deeds of the hero are often exaggerated as are the perils he faces. A good example in *Beowulf* is the description of Beowulf's swimming competition with Breca (ll. 506–89) during which he kills 'niceras nigene' (nine sea-beasts).

Litotes is a figure of speech which uses understatement for effect. It is frequently used in heroic poetry because understating things is an ironic way of emphasising them. For example, the description of the haunted mere ends with the phrase: 'Nis þæt heoru stow!' ('That is not a pleasant place!')

Introduction:

Shared reading of ll. 607–837; pp. 21–7 (15 mins. approx.)

Ask students to find examples of boasting, hyperbole and litotes. Note: there are examples of all three in the passage. The example of boasting is a good one. Beowulf makes his boast before the fight, and afterwards, the poet specifically states that he had fulfilled it. The examples of hyperbole and litotes are less obvious (hyperbole – ll. 771, 790; pp. 25, 26; litotes, ll. 717, 739; p. 24). For more obvious examples, see the swimming competition (ll. 506–89; pp. 18–20).

Development:

1. Students (working in pairs) re-read lines 611–29; p. 21 and discuss and make notes on Wealhtheow and her role.

2. Students (working in pairs) prepare to write a comparison between Beowulf and Grendel by jotting down descriptive words and phrases in a table like the following:

BEOWULF	GRENDEL
battle-fierce warrior	*he bore God's wrath*

Plenary:

Discuss the information retrieved by students. The notes below contain some of they key points:

Wealhtheow is 'queenly', 'dignified', gracious and richly-attired. She is the ideal Anglo-Saxon noblewoman. Anglo-Saxon women enjoyed a position of respect, independence and equality (commensurate with their rank). For example, women could own land and property (Wealhtheow is 'Adorned in *her* gold'). Her role at this feast is to serve the lord and his guests with a symbolic drink of welcome (the drink was mead, which is fermented honey). When Beowulf accepts the drink, he also accepts an obligation to serve her and her lord.

Beowulf is presented as the ultimate Anglo-Saxon warrior hero. He promises to kill Grendel or die himself. He is brave and strong, so strong that he boasts that he will fight him hand to hand, as to fight him with a sword would be unfair.

Grendel is a kind of troll. He is evil, full of anger, and has an ugly light in his eyes. He is very strong – he bursts through the iron-bound door easily. He is hungry for human flesh. He is invulnerable to weapons.

Discuss exactly what happens in the fight.

Homework:

Ask students to write their notes in essay form. Encourage students to include short quotations from the poem using some of the words and phrases they noted down during the lesson. The following is a suggested outline:

* Briefly describe Wealhtheow, the welcome ceremony and Beowulf's boasting speech.

* Describe the character of Beowulf.

* Describe Grendel, including the violent way he kills and eats Hondscioh (the man's name is given later in the poem).

* Describe the fight between Beowulf and Grendel.

Follow-up:

Investigate boasting today both at school and in the media.

The Haunted Mere

Unit 2: Lesson 3

70 minutes approx.

Word/Sentence Activity:

Explain the following features of the Anglo-Saxon language which will be used later in the lesson:

Spelling

Anglo-Saxon spelling uses the following symbols which are not used in the modern alphabet:

æ = *a* (short *a* as in *hat* – *a* is a long vowel pronouced either *ay* or *ah*)

ð and þ = *th*

Pronunciation

A phonetic pronunciation of the text will give reasonable results. This can be further improved by noting the following:

- final *g* is usually pronounced *y*, e.g. *dæg* (*day*) is pronounced *dæy*

- initial *c* is usually pronounced *ch*, e.g. *cild* (*child*) is pronounced *chilled*

- the *ge-* prefix is always pronounced *yeh.*

If time allows, play students some examples of spoken Anglo-Saxon. Examples can be found at

http://www.kami.demon.co.uk/gesithas/readings/readings.html

and

http://www.georgetown.edu/cball/oe/oe-audio.html.

Introduction:

Read aloud the Anglo-Saxon text (resource 12) to the class and ask them to re-read it in pairs taking turns of a few lines in turn. Though all concerned (teacher and students) may feel awkward at first, it is well worth doing for two reasons:

- Reading aloud helps to bring out the similarities with modern English that are disguised by spelling and grammatical inflections.

- It is the only way to appreciate the verse form which is based on patterns of rhythm and alliteration.

Development

In pairs, students work through the tasks at the bottom of the sheet.

Plenary:

Go over the tasks on resource 12.

Notes:
Identifying alliteration is easy, but it is rather more difficult to identify the rhythm pattern due to the strangeness of the language. However, some students may have done this well enough to discover the basic pattern of Anglo-Saxon poetry:

- Four stressed syllables in each line, but with a variable number of unstressed syllables.

- Each line is divided into two half-lines linked by alliteration.

- Alliteration on two or three of the first three stresses.

As in any long poem, the pattern is treated with great flexibility to avoid monotony.

The harder one looks, the more words there are which are similar to modern English. For example, *lond = land*, is fairly obvious, but *næssas = cliffs* also has a link with modern English in the word *ness = headland* (OED).

There are many effective adjectives, e.g. *secret* land, *windy* cliffs, *dangerous* fen.

The litotes in the last line is highly effective after the passage of horrific description.

Homework:

Students write their own description of the haunted mere in prose. Encourage them to develop and extend the description. For example, Tolkien's description of the lake outside the Doors of Moria may have been inspired by the description of the haunted mere (*The Fellowship of the Ring*, ISBN 0048231851, pp. 393–402).

Follow-up:

Compare the literal translation and Heaney's translation with other translations (many are available – see web address in the footnote to the Unit plan for two very different versions).

In a subsequent lesson, study Beowulf's fight with Grendel's Mother, ll. 383–650; pp. 46–53.

12. The Haunted Mere (ll. 1357–72; p. 45)

NOTE: Letters not used in modern English: æ = a (as in 'hat'), ð and þ = 'th'

ANGLO-SAXON TEXT WITH GLOSSES	LITERAL TRANSLATION
Hie dygel lond They secret land	They guard a secret land
warigeað, wulfhleoþu, windige næssas, guard wolf-slope windy cliffs	of wolf slopes, windy cliffs;
frecne fengelad, ðær fyrgenstream dangerous fen path there mountain stream	a dangerous fen path where a mountain stream
under næssa genipu niþer gewiteð, under cliffs darkness downward goes	goes down in darkness under the cliffs;
flod under foldan. Nis þæt feor heonon flood under earth is not far hence	a flood under the earth. It is not far from
milgemearces þæt se mere standeð; by the mile that the mere stands	there, by the mile, that the mere lies.
ofer þæm hongiað hrinde bearwas, over it hangs frosty grove	Over it hangs a frosty grove.
wudu wyrtum fæst wæter oferhelmað. tree roots bound water overshadow	Frost-bound tree roots overshadow the water.
þær mæg nihta gehwæm niðwundor seon, there may night each one evil omen see	There, each night, one may see an evil omen -
fyr on flode. No þæs frod leofað fire on flood no the old one lives	fire on the water. No man living, however old,
gumena bearna, þæt þone grund wite; man son that the bottom knows	knows the bottom [of the mere].
ðeah þe hæðstapa hundum geswenced, although the heath-stepper by hounds chased	Although the heath-stepper chased by hounds,
heorot hornum trum, holtwudu sece, hart horn strong forest seek	the horned hart, may seek [cover] in the forest,
feorran geflymed, ær he feorh seleð, from afar put to flight ere he life give up	put to flight from afar, he would rather give up
aldor on ofre, ær he in wille life on shore ere he will	his life on the shore than hide his head [in the
hafelan hydan. Nis þæt heoru stow! Head hide Is not that pleasant place.	mere]. That is not a pleasant place!

TASKS:

◉ Underline the letters which alliterate in each line of the Anglo-Saxon text.

◉ Try to count the number of stressed syllables in lines 2–4.

◉ From the above, try to work out the pattern of the verse form.

◉ Highlight words which are similar to modern English (don't be put off by unusual spellings and look for words within words).

◉ Highlight adjectives (in the translation and the Anglo-Saxon text).

◉ Find an example of litotes (understatement).

◉ Compare the literal translation with Heaney's translation (p. 45).

Beowulf's Fight with the Dragon

Unit 2: Lesson 4

70 minutes approx.

Objectives

Word: Wd7 recognise layers of meaning in the writer's choice of words, e.g. *kennings*.

Sentence: Sn11 investigate ways English has changed over time and identify current trends of language change, e.g. *links between Anglo-Saxon and Modern English.*

Reading: Rd12 analyse and discuss the use made of rhetorical devices in a text.

Writing: Wr8 Write within the discipline of different poetic forms, exploring how form contributes to meaning, *e.g. the Anglo-Saxon alliterative line.*

Word/Sentence Activity:

Introduce the term *kenning*.

A *kenning* is a kind of metaphor frequently used in Anglo-Saxon and other Nordic (e.g. Old Norse) poetry. It usually consists of two nouns which describe something in a poetic way, for example:

wave steed = ship; whale's road = sea; battle-snake = sword

Introduction:

Shared reading of lines 2510–891; pp. 79–91 (20 mins. approx.)

Development:

In pairs, students work through the questions on resource 13.

Plenary:

Go over the questions on resource 13. Note: four of the first five questions are aimed at developing students' understanding of the Anglo-Saxon heroic code (which was general among pre-Christian Germanic and Nordic tribes). Basically, loyalty to the leader is the most highly-prized quality. The leader earns the loyalty of his followers by giving gifts of armour, land and other valuables. The follower repays this by service – usually in battle. Beowulf's followers desert him in his hour of need, all except Wiglaf. As a result, they and their families are punished by exile.

Poetry: many kennings are used to describe the dragon and it is vividly described in many other ways. There are several examples of boasts, for example, Beowulf's boast in line 2524; p. 80, ('I won't shift a foot'). Students will find it quite easy to identify the alliteration in the original text (remind them that it is sounds, not letters, that alliterate, and that all vowels are considered to alliterate). The stresses will be harder for them to identify because of their unfamiliarity with the language. Remind students of the basic pattern of Anglo-Saxon poetry (see Lesson 3).

Homework:

Ask students to write an essay on Beowulf's fight with the dragon using the questions on resource 13 as a starting point. Encourage them to quote both from the translation and the sample of the original text on resource 12.

Follow-up:

In a subsequent single lesson, play the Comitatus game at:
http://www.calhoun-city.k12.ga.us/chs/english/Comitatus.html.
This site describes how to play the game in class (it does not require internet access, or any special resources). The game will reinforce one of the key points in the above lesson. Note: 'comitatus' is the Latin name for a warrior band of the kind described in *Beowulf*.

The Black Beowulf Project
In his introduction, Seamus Heaney explains how the poem helped him to find his own roots. This is possible because of the universality of the poem. Inspired by this, I worked with a group of Afro-Caribbean students to create a black version of *Beowulf*. This turned out to be an exciting project. We soon found many cultural similarities, e.g. the tribal unit, warriorhood, a respect for ancestors. The students looked for a historical background which was analagous to the Scandinavian background to the poem, and eventually settled on the Zulu nation, partly because of its warrior culture, and partly because it is one of the best documented. They researched the geneaology of chiefs, burial customs, fighting techniques, weapons, clothing, religion, culture and mythology. The next step was to weave all this into the poem, which was re-written in black English (see resource 14). At the time of writing, the project is two-thirds complete, but the project is currently held up because Zulu mythology has no equivalent to the dragon. Students are now researching the mythologies of neighbouring tribes to see if they can find a suitable monster.

The project has been of immense value to the students. Like Seamus Heaney, the poem has helped them to discover their own roots, while at the same time developing an appreciation of *Beowulf* and of the universal values that underlie it. The progress of the Black Beowulf Project can be followed online at: http://www.english-kit-hodder.co.uk

13. Questions on Beowulf's Fight with the Dragon

DISCUSSION & WRITING

Why does Beowulf decide to fight the dragon with sword and armour, instead of bare-handed as he fought Grendel? (ll. 2516–23)

What is the reaction of Beowulf's comrades when they see that he is 'bysigum gebæded' ('hard-pressed in battle')? (ll. 2575–601)

What are Wiglaf's motives for helping Beowulf at great risk to his own life? (ll. 2631–60)

Make a list of the objects in the dragon's hoard (this will be used later to compare with the finds in the burial mound at Sutton Hoo).

What sentence is passed by Wiglaf on Beowulf's cowardly followers? (ll. 2850–91). Do you think this sentence is fair a) in the light of the Anglo-Saxon heroic code? and b) in the light of modern values?

POETRY

Highlight, or make a list, of kennings, adjectives and any other interesting words and phrases which are used to describe the dragon.

Find examples of boasting.

Find examples of litotes (understatement for effect)

In the original text below, highlight alliteration.

In the original text below, highlight stressed syllables (as far as you are able).

BEOWULF (lines 2559–64)		LITERAL TRANSLATION
Biorn under beorge	bordrand onswaf	Man by the barrow, swung his shield towards the strange terror, the lord of the Geats, that was coiled and scaly. Its heart desired to seek battle. Sword had drawn the good war king, his heirloom sword, its edge not dull.
wiðð ðam gryregieste,	Geata dryhten;	
ða wæs hringbogan	heorte gefysed	
sæcce to seceanne.	Sweord ær gebræd	
god guðcyning,	gomele lafe,	
ecgum unslaw.		

14. Black Beowulf

Listun: yous ave eard of da Zulu chiefs
in da old days and ow dey were mighty warrias.
Zulu, da son of Malandela, took many an enemy's kraal,
terrified many a warria, fathered many sons;
A line of chiefs: Punga, Mageba, Ndaba, Jama
and, chief among chiefs, Senzangakhona.
He prospered unda da sky until bruvers everywhere
listened whun he spoke. He was a strong chief!
Senzangakhona did ave a son; a child fa is kraal,
sent by *unKulunkulu to comfort da people,
to keep them from fear – Shaka was is name;
He was famous throughout Zululand.
Young princes should do as he did –
build up da impies while they is still young
so dat whun they're old people will fear them in time of war.
Senzangakhona died at is fated our, went to unKulunkulu still strong.
Is people buried im in a sitting position in is cattle kraal,
sown into the skin of a black bull killed that day.
Shaka ruled da Zulu a long time afta Senzangakhona's death,
and to im was born da wicked Dingane, fierce in ruk,
who ruled until he wa old.

*ancestors

The Monster's Point of View

Unit 2: Lesson 5

70 minutes approx.

> ### Objectives
>
> **Word:** Wd6 know and use the terms that are useful for analysing language, e.g. *person and point of view.*
>
> **Reading:** Rd6 comment on the authorial perspectives offered in texts on individuals, community and society in texts from different cultures.
>
> **Writing:** (not listed) explore authorial perspective by rewriting part of a story from a different point of view.

Note:
John Gardner's *Grendel* is an excellent re-interpretation of the story of Beowulf from the monster's point of view. However, it is not recommended as a whole-class text because of its difficulty. This lesson requires one copy from which the teacher can read to the class. The following lesson is intended for group reading by a group of more able students who will need a copy each.

Word/Sentence Activity:

Revise person and point of view. The best way to do this is to ask students to write out the past tense of the verb 'to be' (past tense because this is the 'story-telling' tense):

	TO BE (PAST TENSE)	
Person	**Singular**	**Plural**
First person:	I was	we were
Second person:	you were	you were
Third person:	*name*/he/she/it was	they were

The first and third person forms are particularly important because they are used to create the 'point of view' in story writing. For example:

> *I was only a boy when the terror began...*
- This story is written from a *first person* point of view.

> *He was only a boy when the terror began...*
- This version of the story is written from a *third person* point of view.

Introduction:

Read chapters 11 and 12. These chapters are a retelling of the story of Beowulf from the monster's point of view from the time of Beowulf's arrival to the monster's death.

Discuss the advantages and limitations of writing this story from a first person point of view.

Development:

Ask students to choose another character in *Beowulf* and to retell the story from his, her or its point of view. Encourage students to explore the thoughts and feelings of the subject in the same way that Gardner explored Grendel's. Students can choose any subject from the following:

Hrothgar	Grendel's Mother
Wealtheow	The Dragon
Unferth	Wiglaf

Plenary:

Share work done so far and discuss how the same events can look very different from another character's point of view.

Homework:

Complete the retelling from another character's point of view.

Follow-up:

Some critics have argued that Grendel's language and complexity of thought are out of keeping with the character. Ask students to:

● Find examples of Grendel's use of sophisticated language and complex thinking.

● Discuss whether this is out of character.

Grendel Overview

Unit 2: Lesson 6

70 minutes approx.

Objectives

Reading: Rd18 discuss a substantial prose text, sharing perceptions, negotiating common readings and accounting for differences of view.

Writing: Wr14 make a counter-argument to a view that has been expressed, addressing weaknesses in the argument and offering alternatives.

Speaking and Listening: S&L9 discuss and evaluate conflicting evidence to arrive at a considered viewpoint.

Starter Activity

This lesson is designed for group reading for a group of more able students. They should read the whole book in their own time before doing the following activities.

Word/Sentence Activity:

Revise how to support points in literary essays with evidence from the text by supporting each main point with a reference to the text, either direct (i.e. a quotation) or indirect (i.e. explaining in your own words what the text says) (see resource 41, in Unit 5, Lesson 1).

The main types of evidence about characters are:

- How the author describes the characters.
- What characters do.
- What characters say.
- What other characters say about them.

Introduction:

Students work through the discussion questions on resource 15, 'Grendel' Tasks. Note that the discussion questions are matched to the written tasks, so that there is an opportunity to explore each of the characters in discussion as a preparation for writing.

Development:

Each student chooses one of the characters to write about in detail.

Plenary:

Share ideas about the discussion questions.

Homework:

Students finish the essays on their chosen characters.

Follow-up:

The poet Robert Browning tried something similar to John Gardner when he wrote a poem from Caliban's point of view: 'Caliban upon Setebos'. Caliban is a similar sort of creature to Grendel – half-human, half troll – however, he is much less sinister. This poem can be found online at: http://users.mhc.edu/facultystaff/jpierce/fall99/eng201/caliban.html

15. 'Grendel' Tasks

DISCUSSION:

- 'Violence and shame have lined the old man's face with mysterious calm' (p. 121). What were Hrothgar's achievements as a young king, and how did Grendel bring him to his present state?

- 'He reshapes the world' (p. 49). What is the role of the 'scop' (poet or minstrel) in Anglo-Saxon society? What role does he have in 'Grendel'?

- 'We see from the mountaintop: all time, all space' (p. 63). How is the dragon's view of the world different from that of 'low creatures'? Why did Grendel want to see the dragon and what does he learn from it?

- 'I've never seen a live hero before.' (p. 84). What does Unferth understand by the term 'hero'? Why does Grendel think the idea of a hero is laughable?

- 'She'd lain aside her happiness for theirs.' (p. 104). Explore Wealtheow's role as a 'peace-weaver'. Why does Grendel decide not to kill her?

- 'Their leader was as big as a mountain' (p. 153). Compare the character of Beowulf as developed by Gardner with the character in the original poem.

WRITING:

Choose one of the characters listed below and write a two-part essay.

Part 1: what we learn about the character from *Beowulf*.
Part 2: how John Gardner develops the character.

Characters:

- Grendel (Chs 1 & 2 – and, of course, the rest of the book!)

- Hrothgar (Chs 3 & 8)

- The Shaper (the poet/minstrel – from Anglo-Saxon 'scop')
  (Chs 3–4)

- The Dragon (Ch 5 and the first two paragraphs of 6)

- Unferth (Ch 6)

- Wealtheow (Ch 7)

- Beowulf

Sutton Hoo

Unit 2: Lesson 7

70 minutes approx.

Objectives

Sentence: Sn5 evaluate their ability to shape ideas rapidly into cohesive paragraphs *which relate to the requirements of specific tasks.*

Reading: Rd6 comment on the authorial perspectives offered in texts on individuals, community and society in texts from different cultures.

Writing: Wr9 integrate diverse information into a coherent and comprehensive account.

Word/Sentence Activity:

Explain to students that many non-fiction texts are non-chronological, i.e. they are not organised by time sequence. In a text like 'The Sutton Hoo Burial' it is possible to arrange the information in many different ways. Students can explore this for themselves in activity A, below.

Non-fiction paragraphs usually begin with a *topic sentence*. This is the sentence which states what the paragraph is about. The topic sentence is developed by examples or explanation. Students can explore this in activity B, below.

Introduction:

Explain to students that the archaeological finds at Sutton Hoo in 1939 brought the world of Beowulf to life. The finds were dated to the early seventh century, which is the approximate date of the oral composition of the poem.

Shared reading of resource 16, The Sutton Hoo Ship Burial, will provide students with further information.

If time allows, students could explore the text further by:

A. Cutting up the text by paragraph and seeing how well the text reads when the paragraphs are put together in a different order.

B. Highlighting the topic sentences in some of the paragraphs. Examine how each paragraph is developed with examples or explanation.

C. Comparing the description of this find with their list of treasures found in the dragon's hoard in *Beowulf* (see Lesson 4).

Development:

Students play the Sutton Hoo card game in groups of 3–4. The cards (preferably cut out in advance, and mounted and laminated if possible) are shuffled and placed face down in the centre of the table. Each student takes it in turn to find the passage referred to on the card and read it to the rest of the group.

A more advanced version of the game can be played by more able students, after a period of extended study of the text, or after playing the version above. For this version another set of cards has to be prepared without references to the text. Students then have to find their own passages to match the picture on the card. If they are able to do this, they keep the card, if not, they put it back at the bottom of the pack. Play continues until all the cards have been won.

Plenary:

Discuss what students should have learned from the game, i.e. that many of the archeological finds are close representations of their counterparts in the poem. For example, the burial itself is similar to the burials described in *Beowulf*, and the treasure hoard is similar to the dragon's treasure hoard which is also in a barrow. The helmet, with its face mask, is similar to the description of Wiglaf's helmet – 'under here-griman' ('under his battle-mask').

Homework:

Write an essay which relates the finds at Sutton Hoo to Beowulf.

Follow-up:

Students should try to see colour photographs of the Sutton Hoo finds, either in the school library or at:

http://www.britainexpress.com/History/sutton-hoo.htm

16. The Sutton Hoo Ship Burial

In 1939 archaeologists unearthed an astonishing Anglo-Saxon ship burial in Woodbridge, Suffolk; astonishing both for the state of preservation of the objects within the tomb, but also astonishing for the sheer rich quality of the artifacts.

The burial goods from Sutton Hoo are remarkable – gold weapons and armour, inlaid ornaments, silver and tableware. Also found with the body was a purse containing 37 gold Merovingian (Gaulish) gold coins dating from about AD 620.

The armour at Sutton Hoo appears to be Swedish, or at least it is made in the Swedish style. Certainly the custom of ship burials is a Nordic one – there are many similar Viking remains in Denmark and Sweden. There is also a large silver dish made in Byzantium about AD 500 and a set of 10 silver bowls from the Mediterranean.

Who was buried at Sutton Hoo? Who was so powerful in his lifetime to be interred with ceremony in a ship nearly 90 feet in length surrounded by so much golden splendor? Conjecture focuses on Redwald, a Saxon 'bretwalda', or King, of East Anglia.

According to the Venerable Bede in his 'Ecclesiastical History', Redwald ruled East Anglia in 616, although his power may have stretched as far north as the Humber. Redwald was the first East Anglian king to pay any heed to Christianity. He may have converted to the new religion – certainly his successors were Christian.

Archaeologists have reconstructed how the burial at Sutton Hoo must have taken place. A long trench was dug atop a 100 ft. high cliff above the river Deben. The ship was dragged up from the river and set in the trench. A hut was built in the centre of the ship, and there was placed a large coffin and the grave goods. The trench was then filled in and a large mound erected over the top.

When the ship was uncovered the timbers had rotted away. However, the rivets still remained, and the rotting timbers had stained the sand, so the pattern of boat construction could be determined, and a good picture of the boat emerged. It was about 90 feet long and 14 feet wide, with a high bow and stern. It is easily the largest Anglo-Saxon ship ever discovered.

The importance of Sutton Hoo cannot be overstated. From the grave goods we can learn a lot about the pattern of life in this darkest part of the Dark Ages in Britain. Even the style of the craftsmanship lets us draw conclusions about how strong Saxon connections were with rest of Europe.

In this case it seems clear that there was a strong Norse influence in East Anglia, but also ties to Gaul and the Mediterranean. Clearly, trade with those areas was maintained throughout these troubled times.

The goods discovered at Sutton Hoo are on display at the British Museum in London.

source: http://www.britainexpress.com/History/sutton-hoo.htm

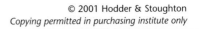

17. Sutton Hoo Cards

BURIAL MOUND	SHIP	TREASURE HOARD
	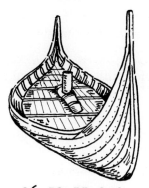	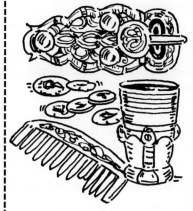
3137 – end; pp. 98–9 (Beowulf's funeral)	26–52; pp. 3–4 (Scyld's funeral); 198–228 p. 9 (Beowulf sets sail)	2231–66; pp. 71–2 (The dragon's treasure hoard)
HELMET	SWORD	SHIELD

2515–55; pp. 79–80 (Beowulf prepares to fight the dragon) 2602–19; p. 82 (Wiglaf helps)	1455 – 64; p. 48 (Hrunting); 1557–83; p. 51 (A giant's sword); 2556–85; p.81 (an hierloom sword)	2669–76; p. 84 (Wiglaf's shield burned to the boss)
STANDARD	LYRE	DRINKING HORNS
	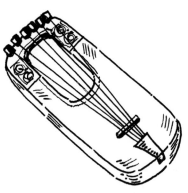	
1020–34; p. 33 (Hrothgar rewards Beowulf) 2756–71; p. 87 (the dragon's hoard)	86–101; p. 5 (The song of Creation); 1063–68; pp. 34 – 9 (The lay of Finn)	602–30; p. 21 (Wealtheow serves mead); 1159–74; p. 39 (Celebrating Grendel's death)

The Rune Poem

Unit 2: Lesson 8

70 minutes approx.

Objectives

Reading: Rd16 analyse ways in which different cultural contexts and traditions have influenced language and style.

Speaking and Listening: S&L3 develop interview techniques which include planning a series of linked questions, helping the respondent to give useful answers, responding to and extending the responses.

Word/Sentence Activity:

Use resource 18 'Anglo-Saxon runes' to introduce students to the runic alphabet and to explore the limitations of the alphabet in representing spoken sounds.

Introduction:

Explain to students that runes are a primitive form of writing used mainly for inscriptions on stone, wood and metal, e.g. some sword blades have runic inscriptions. Runes also acquired a magical significance. This is probably because the act of reading and writing seemed magical to the illiterate and because runes were also used to tell fortunes. The Rune Poem probably had two purposes: as a teaching aid for the FUTHORK (the runic alphabet, named after the first six letters) and as a fortune-teller's guide.

Continue with shared reading of The Rune Poem (resource 19) as a poem.

Development:

Students play the fortune-telling game by cutting out the rune cards. Note: some students who are members of certain religions may need to be excused from this lesson (consult school and LEA policy). In any case, it is important to emphasise that the fortune telling game is 'just for fun', like reading a horoscope in the newspaper.

There are two ways to read fortunes. The simple method is to ask the enquirer to select a card from the pack at random (for interpretation, see below). A more interesting way (which also teaches students to write with runes) is to spell out a person's given name (Christian/first) in runes and to interpret it a letter at a time.

Interpretation

The person doing the interpretation has to pick up ideas from the description of the rune in the verse, and use his/her intuition to shape it into a personal reading. Thus, if the rune Nyd was drawn, the fortune-teller might say something like:

> You are unhappy because you want something badly. But don't worry, someone has seen your need and will come to help you.

An alternative activity (to be used if the above activity would not be suitable for the cultural make-up of the class) is for students to practise writing using runes.

Plenary:

Discuss what we can learn from the poem about the Anglo-Saxon way of life, values and beliefs.

Notes:

Feoh and Gifu show the high value placed on generosity.

Ger shows the importance of harvest in an agricultural society.

Peorth refers to the joys of the mead hall.

Eh shows the value put upon horses.

Man shows a sadly negative view of human nature.

Ger, Man and Daeg have Christian references, though the rest of the poem is set in a pagan warrior culture.

Poetry:

There are some vivid kennings, e.g. sea-steed (ship), fishes bath (sea), gannet's bath (sea). In Lagu, the 'sea-steed' is developed into an extended metaphor with 'bridle'.

Is – note the poetic description, the hard onomatopoeic sounds (even better in the original: 'glisnaþ glæshlutter, glimman gelicust') and the two similes.

Homework:

Ask students to produce written versions of their predictions.

Follow-up:

This translation, side by side with the Anglo-Saxon original, may be found at: http://w3.one.net/~tomwulf/NW/OE/RunePoem.html

Some students may be interested in reading the original text. There are also some useful notes on the poem:

www.geocities.com/TimesSquare/4948/runes/ – inc fonts

18. Anglo-Saxon Runes

RUNES	NAMES	SOUNDS	RUNES	NAMES	SOUNDS
	Feoh	f		Sigel	s
	Ur	u/v		Tir	t
	Thorn	th		Beorc	b
	Os	o		Eh	e
	Rad	r		Man	m
	Cen	c/k		Lagu	l
	Gifu	g		Ing	ng
	Wen	w		Ethel	oe/ee
	Haegl	h		Daeg	d
	Nyd	n		Ac	long a
	Is	i		Aesc	short a
	Ger	j		Yr	y
	Eoh	long I		Iar	gh
	Peorth	p		Ear	ea
	Eolhx	x/z			

TASKS:

Write out the modern alphabet and try to match each letter with a rune. Write down any problems you had.

Write some short messages in runes. Try to use the runes fully, e.g. words beginning with 'th' should be written with the rune Thorn.

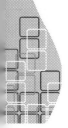

---

19. The Rune Poem

RUNE	NAME	MEANING	SOUND
ᚠ	Feoh	Wealth is a comfort to every man, Although each should share it freely, To gain the approval of the Lord.	f
ᚢ	Ur	Aurochs is a courageous beast, having huge horns, A savage beast, it fights with its horns, A noble moor-stepper, it is a fierce beast!	u/v
ᚦ	Thorn	Thorn is extremely sharp, Painful to any thane that grasps it, Immeasurably fierce to any man, That rests among them.	th
ᚩ	Os	Mouth is the source of every statement, Wisdom's support and a comfort to the wise, And the joy and delight of the nobleman.	o
ᚱ	Rad	Riding is to the warrior in the hall easy, But very strenuous for one who sits on top, Of a powerful horse over the long miles.	r
ᚳ	Cen	Torch is to the living, known by its fire, Shining and bright, most often it burns inside, Where princes sit at ease.	c/k
ᚷ	Gifu	Generosity is a mark of distinction and praise for men, A prop to their honor and for the wretched, A benefit and a means of survival, when there is no other.	g
ᚹ	Wen	He has Joy, who knows little of the woes of pain or sorrow, And has for himself, prosperity and happiness, And also the contentment of a fortified town.	w
ᚻ	Haegl	Hail is the whitest of grains, whirling from heaven's height, Gusts of wind toss it about, and then it becomes water.	h
ᚾ	Nyd	Need oppresses the heart, Yet often it becomes for the sons of men, A source of help and salvation, If they heed it in time.	n
ᛁ	Is	Ice is very cold, and immeasurably slippery, It glitters, clear as glass, very like jewels, A floor, wrought by frost, fair to behold.	l

Continued

RUNE	NAME	MEANING	SOUND
	Ger	Harvest is a joy to men, when God, heaven's holy king, Causes the earth to produce bright fruits, For both the rich and the poor.	j
	Eoh	Yew is a tree, rough on the outside, Hard and firm in the earth, guardian of fires, Supported by roots, a joy on the estate.	long i
	Peorth	Lot-cup is recreation and laughter to the high spirited ... For the warriors gathered happily together in the mead hall.	p
	Eolhx	Elk-sedge is usually found in the fens, Growing on the water, Grimly wounding, Staining with blood, any man who grasps it.	x/z
	Sigel	Sun is always hope for seamen, When they row the sea-stead over the fishes bath, Until it brings them to land.	s
	Tir	Tir is one of the guiding signs, It keeps faith well with noblemen, Ever it holds on course, through cloudy night And never fails.	t
	Beorc	Birch is void of fruit, Nevertheless it bears shoots without seed, It is beautiful by its branches, High of crown, fairly adorned, Tall and leafy, touching the heights.	b
	Eh	Horse is a joy for princes among the noble, A steed prou in its hooves, when warriors Prosperous on horseback exchange speech concerning it, And it is always a comfort to the restless.	e
	Man	Man rejoicing in life is beloved by his kinsmen Yet everyone shall betray another, Because the Lord wills it by his judgement, To commit that wretched flesh to the earth.	m
	Lagu	Water seems to be unending to men, If they are obliged to venture out on a tossing ship, And the sea waves terrify them exceedingly, And the sea-steed does not heed the bridle.	l
	Ing	Ing was first among the East Danes, Beheld by men, until afterwards to the east, He went over the waves, (his) chariot ran after, Then the warriors named the hero thusly.	ng

Continued

RUNE	NAME	MEANING	SOUND
	Ethel	The ancestral estate is very dear to every man, If he may there in his house enjoy most often in prosperity, That which is right and fitting.	oe/ee
	Daeg	Day is sent by the Lord, beloved of man, Glorious light of the Creator, joy and hope, To those who have and have not, of benefit to all.	d
	Ac	Oak is the nourishment of meat on the earth, For the children of men; often it travels, Over the gannet's bath – the spear-sea tests, Whether the oak keeps faith nobly.	long a
	Aesc	The ash is very tall, dear to mankind, Strong in its position, it holds its ground rightly, Though many men attack it.	short a
	Yr	Yew is a joy and honor to all princes and nobles, And is fair on a mount, reliable on a journey, A type of army gear.	y
	Iar	Eel is a river fish, and yet it takes its food on land, It has a beautiful dwelling place, surrounded by water, There it lives in delight.	gh
	Ear	Earth is loathsome to every nobleman. When irresistibly the flesh, The dead body, begins to grow cold, The livid one chooses the earth for a bedmate, Fruits fail, joys vanish, covenants are broken.	ea

UNIT 3: MACBETH

Title of unit: MACBETH

Resources
Books: Any edition of the play
Film: *Macbeth*, Roman Polanski, 1971

Year: 9	Term: 3, first half	Duration: 8 lessons	Set: All

NLS objectives		NC objectives
Roman Polanski's *Macbeth* 1 and 2	Rd8, Wr13, S&L13	En1 4c) appreciate how the structure and organisation of scenes and plays contribute to dramatic effect.
Is Macbeth a Capricorn?	Wd7, Sn4, Rd15, Wr13, S&L13	En1 6e) dialect variation.
Psychoanalyse Lady Macbeth	Wd7, Sn7, Rd14, Wr13, S&L13	En2 5c) how the nature and purpose of media products influence content and meaning.
The Supernatural in Macbeth	Wd7, Sn7, Rd12, Wr13 S&L5	En2 8a i) two plays by Shakespeare, one of which should be studied in KS3.
Fate	Sn7, Rd6, Wr16, S&L9	En3 1 writing to analyse, review, comment.
Holinshed's *Chronicles of Scotland*	Sn11, Rd2, Wr16, S&L9	
The Ballad O' Mackbeth	Sn10, Rd7, S&L7	

Teaching sequence	Outcomes
Week 1: Roman Polanski's *Macbeth* 1 and 2	Make notes on the film. *Write a review of the film.
Week 2: Is Macbeth a Capricorn? Psychoanalyse Lady Macbeth	*Essay on the character of Macbeth. *Psychoanalyst's report or essay on Lady Macbeth.
Week 3: The Curse of the Play Fate	*Write about the theme of evil in the play. *Write about fate and free will in Macbeth.
Week 4: Holinshed's *Chronicles of Scotland* The Ballad O'Mackbeth	*Write about Shakespeare's use of sources. Write a summary of the play.
	Assessment pieces

Notes:
Resources for teaching *Macbeth* abound. The purpose of this unit is twofold: to provide resources which cover the plot, characters, themes and language in the play, and at the same time to offer approaches to the play which are different (or at least, approaches which have not been overdone) so that they can be used alongside other resources as complementary materials.

The teachers' notes give recommended readings to prepare for the focus of the lesson, but students will, of course, need to read the whole play. Ideally, this should be done before starting these lessons.

Macbeth is a relatively easy play for students to read and understand. However, some students may benefit from reading the modernised version of *Macbeth* at http://www.cln.org/themes/macbeth.html

Roman Polanski's Macbeth

Unit 3: Lessons 1 & 2

70 minutes approx.

Objectives

Word: (not listed) appreciate the specific meaning in context of an increasing range of words e.g. *media studies terms*.

Reading: Rd8 analyse how media texts influence and are influenced by readers.

Writing: Wr13 present a case persuasively enough to gain the attention and influence the responses of a specified group of readers.

Speaking and Listening: S&L13 develop and compare different interpretations of scenes or plays by Shakespeare or other dramatists.

Word/Sentence Activity:

Teach the following media studies terms:

Binary oppositions – patterns of opposites in a text, e.g. light and dark, good and evil, etc.
Signified – what a sign or symbol stands for (see below).
Signifier – the sign or symbol itself. Road signs, words, maps, logos, flags are all signifiers.
Symbol – something that stands for something else, e.g. the union flag is a symbol that stands for the United Kingdom.

Ask students to think of their own examples of signs and symbols, and in each case identify the signifier and the signified.

Introduction:

Roman Polanski's, classic film *Macbeth* (1971) can be used as an introduction to the play or as a way of looking at the play from another angle.

Divide the film into two showings, one per lesson.

Development:

During the showings of the film use the Film Analysis Checklists (resources 20 and 21). Note that the checklist is designed to take film analysis one step further than in Year 8. For this reason, the first two sections in Part A are concerned with semiological analysis (the necessary skills are covered in the starter activity). The two Film Language resources from the Year 8 book can be used to support section 3 of Part A.

This can be used in a number of ways:

- Students use and make notes on Part A during the first showing and on Part B during the second.

- A modified version of the checklist can be created by omitting some sections and expanding others.

- Note that the checklist is intended for notetaking. The categories can then be used as a template for an essay.

Plenary:

After each showing, discuss the notes that students have written on the Film Analysis Checklists.

Notes on Checklist part A:
Discuss some of the signifiers, opposites and film language that students may have identified, for example:

SIGNIFIER	SIGNIFIED
the three witches	evil/supernatural
noose, severed hand, dagger	black magic/Macbeth's future
crown	kingship
captain covered in blood	fresh from battle/honour
medallion	thane of Cawdor

BINARY OPPOSITES	
fair	foul
good	evil
peace	war

LANGUAGE OF FILM
Long shot of bleak landscape. Close up of witch's staff scraping a circle in the sand. Zoom out to show another witch helping to dig out the circle. Continue zooming out to mid shot of all three witches. Cut to mid shot of seagull flying overhead. Cut to close up of hangman's noose, cut to mid shot of three witches. Cut to close up of severed hand holding dagger...etc.

Discuss how these can increase our understanding of the play.

Notes on Checklist part B:
Roman Polanski's direction is generally regarded as excellent. Most critics accept that this is the best film version of *Macbeth* to date (however, see the follow-up section for a different view). The script – often the weakest point in many modern films – is of course by Shakespeare. The film seems to be well cast and acted. Music, costumes and locations are all highly effective. With regard to the final section, the best way to evaluate the film is to compare it to another version.

Homework:

After the second lesson, write a review of the film, using resources 20 and 21 (Film Analysis Checklist Parts 1 and 2) as a basis.

Follow-up:

Read other reviews of the film. An example of a positive review can be found at:
http://www.asn-ibk.ac.at/schulen/borg-ibk/shakespeare/10_Macbeth.html

A reviewer who found the film less successful can be found at:
http://www.epinions.com/mvie-review-15FC-2965FCA-393190AF-prod5

20. Film Analysis Checklist (Part A)

A. DETAILS OF FILM

B. IDENTIFY THE MAIN SIGNIFIERS (SYMBOLS) IN THE FILM

SIGNIFIER	SIGNIFIED

C. LIST BINARY OPPOSITES

D. COMMENT ON THE LANGUAGE OF FILM

What kind of shots, camera angles and editing techniques have been used?

21. Film Analysis Checklist (Part B)

E. PRODUCTION PROCESSES

Direction

Script

Casting

Acting

Music

Costume

Locations

Special Effects

F. OTHER

Any important feature not listed above, e.g. comparison with original if based on a novel or play, etc.

G. OVERALL EVALUATION

Is Macbeth a Capricorn?

Unit 3: Lesson 3

70 minutes approx.

Objectives

Word: Wd7 recognise layers of meaning in the writer's choice of words, e.g. *Shakespeare's use of rhyming verse.*

Sentence: Sn4 integrate speech, reference and quotation effectively into what they write.

Reading: Rd15 extend their understanding of literary heritage by relating major writers to their historical context, and explaining their appeal over time.

Writing: Wr13 present a case persuasively enough to gain the attention and influence the responses of a specified group of readers.

Speaking and Listening: S&L13 develop and compare different interpretations of scenes or plays by Shakespeare or other dramatists.

Starter Activity:

Shakespeare frequently uses rhyming verse in his plays, e.g. for songs. In *Macbeth* he uses rhyming verse in octosyllable couplets (lines with eight syllables and four stresses which rhyme in pairs) for the witches' chants.

Shakespeare also uses rhyme to indicate the end of a scene.

Ask students to:

◉ Count the syllables and stresses in the lines of the witches' chants.

◉ Find examples of a rhyme used to mark the end of a scene.

Introduction:

Explain to students that Shakespeare knew a great deal about astrology and that he may have studied it at Stratford-upon-Avon Grammar School (in those days, astrology was a respectable subject). The basis of astrology is that human personality is influenced by the position of the planets in the zodiac at the time of birth. As a budding playwright, it was probably the twelve different types of personality represented by twelve signs of the zodiac that most interested Shakespeare.

The emphasis in real astrology (as opposed to the journalistic variety) is on character. Predictions of the future are based on comparing the position of the planets at the time of the subject's birth, with their position at a date in the future. Thus, the influence of personality on 'what happens' is very important. It is for this reason that the only accurate horoscopes are based on individual readings.

Shared reading of: Act 1, Sc. III, l. 89 – Act 1, Sc. IV, l. 58, and (if time allows) Act 1, Sc. VII.

Development:

Read resource 22, Is Macbeth a Capricorn?, then, in the second column, make notes about how far Macbeth's character fits the description of a typical Capricorn using evidence from the text.

Plenary:

Discuss how far Macbeth has the characteristics of a typical Capricorn.

The similarities between the Capricorn character and Macbeth are many and thus it seems probable that Shakespeare had this zodiac sign in mind when creating the character of Macbeth.

Homework:

Write an essay on the character of Macbeth. This can be based on this lesson (see suggested outline below) or can be a more general character description which includes a reference to the ideas explored in this lesson.

- Introduction – give a *brief* explanation of astrology and an account of the main characteristics of Capricorns.

- Using your notes, discuss how closely the character of Macbeth is modelled on Capricorn characteristics.

- Which of these characteristics led to Macbeth's downfall?

- What external factors led to Macbeth's downfall?

Follow-up:

Ask students to explore how far other characters in the play fit zodiac characteristics (a summary of characteristics of people born in each zodiac sign can be found in the *Key Stage 3 English Kit: Year 7* page 128). Note: Lady Macbeth seems to be another Capricorn, but we do not know enough about the other characters to make any clear decisions. However, the process of investigating this will help students to learn more about the characters!

22. Is Macbeth a Capricorn?

CAPRICORN TRAITS	MACBETH'S TRAITS
The sign of the goat *December 22nd to January 20th* *Ruling Planet: Saturn* Capricorns are very career-orientated people. They are very ambitious and make determined and resourceful managers. They respect discipline and demand it of those beneath them. They want to be respected and will work hard to achieve this. However, in some Capricorns, this trait can develop into an excessive self-love. Capricorns always have a bit of a doom and gloom as they are pessimists. This trait is particularly noticeable if they feel that they are failing to achieve their ambitions. In extreme cases, this can lead to classic symptoms of manic depression, e.g. ecstatic happiness alternating with deep misery. These mood swings are well described by the adjective linked to their name – *capricious*. Capricorns are deep thinkers. They are rational and logical and often use these abilities to lure their enemies into traps. Many Capricorns, despite their rational minds, develop an interest in the occult which can sometimes become obsessive. Capricorns make few good friends, but are intensely loyal to the few that they have. They make faithful married partners, and once married, they stay married for life. Suitable occupations are: accountants, bankers, estate agents, or management roles in any occupation. Whatever their career choice, they like to get to the top. Capricorn governs the knees, bones and skin, so Capricorns are prone to problems in these areas, e.g. fractures and skin diseases. They are also prone to worry.	

Psychoanalyse Lady Macbeth

Unit 3: Lesson 4

70 minutes approx.

Objectives

Word: Wd7 recognise layers of meaning in the writer's choise of words, e.g. *Shakespeare's use of prose.*

Sentence: Sn7 analyse and exploit the stylistic conventions of the main text types.

Reading: Rd14 analyse the language, form and dramatic impact of scenes and plays by published dramatists.

Writing: Wr13 present a case persuasively enough to gain the attention and influence the responses of a specified group of readers.

Speaking and Listening: S&L13 develop and compare different interpretations of scenes or plays by Shakespeare or other dramatists.

Word/Sentence Activity:

Shakespeare sometimes uses prose (ordinary writing) in his plays. This is usually for comic or lower-class characters, but it can also be used to create a contrast. Ask students to find examples of prose in *Macbeth* and to comment on why Shakespeare has used prose at these points.

Notes:

- The porter speaks in prose in Act II, Sc. III. This is partly because he is a lower-class character, and partly to show that he is drunk and his speech is rambling.

- Lady Macbeth speaks in prose in Act V, Sc. I. This is to emphasise her madness by making her speak in a different way.

Introduction:

Explain that this lesson explores the character of Lady Macbeth with a particular emphasis on her psychological state. Of course, the science of psychology was not developed until the nineteenth century, but great writers have shown accurate insight into psychological states long before this. Perhaps the best example is *Oedipus Tyrannus*, the play by Greek dramatist Sophocles, which so accurately describes a psychological state that Freud (the founding father of psychoanalysis) later named the 'Oedipus complex'.

Working in small groups of 3–4, students re-read Act I, Sc. V–VII (the scenes in which Lady Macbeth screws up her courage) and Act V, Sc. I–III (the scenes which show her mental illness).

Development:

In the same groups, students read the description of anxiety disorders on resource 23, 'Psychoanalyse Lady Macbeth' and make notes in the right–hand column which relate the psychological descriptions to evidence from the text.

Students should also discuss:

- What caused Lady Macbeth's mental illness?

- How might it be treated today?

Plenary:

Discuss how far Lady's Macbeth's mental illness can be diagnosed as different kinds of anxiety disorders. Note: there are many other anxiety disorders, e.g. panic disorders and various types of phobia. For reasons of space, only those relevant to Lady Macbeth have been included on the resource sheet. For this reason, students will find that Lady Macbeth shows symptoms of all three anxiety disorders listed. Shakespeare's description of obsessive-compulsive disorder is particularly impressive.

Homework:

Either:
Write a psychoanalyst's report on Lady Macbeth. This could include:

● An account of the events that caused the anxiety disorders.

● A description of the anxiety disorders with close reference to the text.

● A suggested course of treatment (this will require further research).

Or
Write an essay on the character of Lady Macbeth. This could include:

● A brief character sketch outlining her main characteristics.

● An account of how she responds to Macbeth's letter and encourages him to murder Duncan.

● A discussion of how far she is responsible for Macbeth's action.

● An explanation of why she becomes mentally ill.

Follow-up:

Consider the psychological state of other characters in the play, e.g. the porter, MacDuff when he discovers his family have been murdered, etc.

23. Psychoanalyse Lady Macbeth

ANXIETY DISORDERS	LADY MACBETH
Anxiety is a normal reaction to *stress*. It is only considered abnormal when it is out of proportion to any external cause. There are several kinds of *anxiety disorders*. Someone who suffers from *generalised anxiety disorder* lives each day in a state of high tension. He or she suffers from some or all of the following symptoms: inability to relax, disturbed sleep, fatigue, headaches, dizziness and rapid heart rate. He or she continually worries about problems, is unable to concentrate or make decisions, and is constantly expecting disaster. He or she may also experience panic attacks. During these attacks, he or she feels that something dreadful is about to happen. The feeling is accompanied by heart palpitations, faintness and nausea.	
Another type of anxiety disorder is *obsessive-compulsive disorder*. An example of this is a person who is afraid of germs and spends hours every day washing his or her hands. *Obsessions* are persistent unwelcome thoughts, and *compulsions* are irresistible urges to do something. Obsessive thoughts cover a variety of topics, but most often they are concerned with harming oneself or others, fear of contamination, or satisfactory completion of complicated tasks. Sufferers of this disorder realise the senselessness of their compulsions but become anxious if they try to resist them.	
Post-traumatic stress disorder can arise from situations of extreme stress. The major symptoms include feeling numb to the world, with a lack of interest in life and a feeling of estrangement from others; reliving the trauma in dreams; sleep disturbances, and feelings of guilt.	

The Supernatural in Macbeth

Unit 3: Lesson 5

70 minutes approx.

Objectives

Word: Wd7 recognise layers of meaning in the writer's choice of words, e.g. *use of figurative language*.

Sentence: Sn7 analyse and exploit the stylistic conventions of the main text types.

Reading: Rd12 analyse and discuss the use made of rhetorical devices in a text.

Writing: Wr13 present a case persuasively enough to gain the attention and influence the responses of a specified group of readers.

Speaking and Listening: S&L5 compare different points of view that have been expressed, identifying and evaluating differences and similarities.

Word/Sentence Activity:

One feature that makes Shakespeare's language difficult is that his plays are also long poems. It is the figurative language as much as the archaic language that is difficult. However, it is also the source of the richness of Shakespeare's language. Ask students to re-read Act V, Sc. V, ll. 17–28 and to analyse the figurative language.

Notes:
A series of metaphors in which life is compared to a 'brief candle', 'a walking shadow', builds up to the oft-quoted extended metaphor (obviously drawing on Shakespeare's experience) comparing life to 'a poor player'. Another extended metaphor comparing life to 'a tale told by an idiot' follows this. Discuss how this metaphorical language helps us to understand Shakespeare's state of mind.

Introduction:

Shared reading of resource 24, The Curse of the Play.

Development:

Working in groups of 3–4, students discuss the questions at the end of the passage.

The next step is for students to draw up the table of good and evil in the play as explained on the resource sheet.

The research task can be done in a follow-up lesson in the library, or for a subsequent homework.

Plenary:

Macbeth is a stark exploration of evil and this may explain why superstitions have grown up around it. The myth of the curse is interesting, but the important thing is to analyse the evil in the play. Students may have noticed, when drawing up their table of comparisons that good and evil are strongly contrasted throughout the whole play. For example, Duncan is a very good king, Macbeth admits to himself that Duncan's 'virtues will plead like angels' (Act 1, Sc. VII, ll. 18–19). There is also good within Macbeth. Lady Macbeth says his nature is 'too full 'o the milk of human kindness' (Act 1. Sc. V, l. 17). Evil comes from within – as when Lady Macbeth calls upon evil spirits (Act 1 Sc. V. ll. 38–54), and Macbeth's own ambition, but also from without – the influence of the witches and of Lady Macbeth upon Macbeth.

Homework:

Write an essay about the theme of evil in the play. This could include:

● An introduction explaining that the play's focus on evil has given rise to superstitions about the play.

● A brief explanation of Elizabethan beliefs about witches and witchcraft.

● An explanation of Shakespeare's presentation of evil as something that is both external (represented by the witches), and internal in the shape of his own ambitions, and also Lady Macbeth's ambitions (which are external pressures on Macbeth, but which arise from human weakness).

● An account of how Shakespeare highlights the theme of evil by making a strong contrast with good characters (and good qualities in the evil characters) in the play.

Follow-up:

Find out more about contemporary beliefs about witchcraft at:
http://www.kenyon.edu/projects/margin/witch.htm

24. The Curse of the Play

by Robert Faires (abridged)

The lore surrounding *Macbeth* and its supernatural power begins with the play's creation in 1606. According to some, Shakespeare wrote the tragedy to ingratiate himself to King James I, who had succeeded Elizabeth I only a few years before. In addition to setting the play on James's home turf, Scotland, Will chose to give a nod to one of the monarch's pet subjects, demonology (James had written a book on the subject that became a popular tool for identifying witches in the 17th century). Shakespeare incorporated a trio of spell-casting women into the drama and gave them a set of spooky incantations to recite. Alas, the story goes that the spells Will included in Macbeth were lifted from an authentic black-magic ritual and that their public display did not please the folks for whom these incantations were sacred. Therefore, they retaliated with a curse on the show and all its productions.

Those doing the cursing must have got [ed. changed from 'gotten'] an advance copy of the script or caught a rehearsal because legend has it that the play's infamous ill luck set in with its very first performance. John Aubrey, who supposedly knew some of the men who performed with Shakespeare in those days, has left us with the report that a boy named Hal Berridge was to play Lady Macbeth at the play's opening on August 7, 1606. Unfortunately, he was stricken with a sudden fever and died. It fell to the playwright himself to step into the role.

It's been suggested that James was not that thrilled with the play, as it was not performed much in the century after. Whether or not that's the case, when it was performed, the results were often calamitous. In a performance in Amsterdam in 1672, the actor in the title role is said to have used a real dagger for the scene in which he murders Duncan and done the deed for real. The play was revived in London in 1703, and on the day the production opened, England was hit with one of the most violent storms in its history.

As time wore on, the catastrophes associated with the play just kept piling up like Macbeth's victims. At a performance of the play in 1721, a nobleman who was watching the show from the stage decided to get up in the middle of a scene, walk across the stage, and talk to a friend. The actors, upset by this, drew their swords and drove the nobleman and his friends from the theatre. Unfortunately for them, the noblemen returned with the militia and burned the theatre down. In 1775, Sarah Siddons took on the role of Lady Macbeth and was nearly ravaged by a disapproving audience. It was *Macbeth* that was being performed inside the Astor Place Opera House the night of May 10, 1849, when a crowd of more than 10,000 New Yorkers gathered to protest the appearance of British actor William Charles Macready. (He was engaged in a bitter public feud with an American actor, Edwin Forrest.) The protest escalated into a riot, leading the militia to fire into the crowd. Twenty-three people were killed, 36 were wounded, and hundreds were injured. And it was *Macbeth* that Abraham Lincoln chose to take with him on board the River Queen on the Potomac River on the afternoon of April 9, 1865. The president was reading passages aloud to a party of friends, passages which happened to follow the scene in which Duncan is assassinated. Within a week, Lincoln himself was dead by a murderer's hand.

In the last 135 years, the curse seems to have confined its mayhem to theatre people engaged in productions of the play. [Note: examples from 1882–1942 omitted for reasons of space.]

- In 1942, a production headed by John Gielgud suffered three deaths in the cast – the actor playing Duncan and two of the actresses playing the Weird Sisters – and the suicide of the costume and set designer.

- In 1947, actor Harold Norman was stabbed in the swordfight that ends the play and died as a result of his wounds. His ghost is said to haunt the Colliseum Theatre in Oldham, where the fatal blow was struck. Supposedly, his spirit appears on Thursdays, the day he was killed.

- In 1948, Diana Wynyard was playing Lady Macbeth at Stratford and decided to play the sleepwalking scene with her eyes closed; on opening night, before a full audience, she walked right off the stage, falling 15 feet. Amazingly, she picked herself up and finished the show.

- In 1953, Charlton Heston starred in an open-air production in Bermuda. On opening night, when the soldiers storming Macbeth's castle were to burn it to the ground onstage, the wind blew the smoke and flames into the audience, which ran away. Heston himself suffered severe burns in his groin and leg area from tights that were accidentally soaked in kerosene.

- In 1955, Olivier was starring in the title role in a pioneering production at Stratford and during the big fight with Macduff almost blinded fellow actor Keith Michell.

- In a production in St. Paul, Minnesota, the actor playing Macbeth dropped dead of heart failure during the first scene of Act III.

- In 1988, the Broadway production starring Glenda Jackson and Christoper Plummer is supposed to have gone through three directors, five Macduffs, six cast changes, six stage managers, two set designers, two lighting designers, 26 bouts of flu, torn ligaments, and groin injuries. (The numbers vary in some reports.)

- In 1998, in the Off-Broadway production starring Alec Baldwin and Angela Bassett, Baldwin somehow sliced open the hand of his Macduff.

- Add to these the long list of actors, from Lionel Barrymore in the 1920s to Kelsey Grammer just this year, who have attempted the play only to be savaged by critics as merciless as the Scottish lord himself.

For additional reference on the *Macbeth* curse, see Richard Huggett's *Supernatural on Stage: Ghosts and Superstitions in the Theatre* (NY, Taplinger, 1975).

DISCUSSION:

- What is your opinion of the story of the curse on this play? Do you think that the incidents listed above provide worthwhile evidence, or do you think they are a series of coincidences?

WRITING:

- Explore the real nature of evil in the play by drawing up a chart in two columns GOOD – and EVIL – and jotting down words, phrases and events from the place in the appropriate column.

RESEARCH:

- Find out about contemporary beliefs about witches and witchcraft.

To read a complete version of the article including the examples of mishaps that took place from 1882–1942, visit:
http://www.auschron.com/issues/dispatch/2000-10-13/arts_feature2.html

Fate

Unit 3: Lesson 6

70 minutes approx.

Objectives

Sentence: Sn7 analyse and exploit the stylistic conventions of the main text types.

Reading: Rd6 comment on the authorial perspectives offered in texts on individuals, community and society in texts from different cultures.

Writing: Wr16 present a balanced analysis of a situation, text, issue or set of ideas, taking into account a range of evidence and opinions.

Speaking and Listening: S&L9 discuss and evaluate conflicting evidence to arrive at a considered viewpoint.

Word/Sentence Activity:

Explain to students that the form in which Shakespeare's plays are written (apart from songs in verse and short passages in prose) is blank verse. Blank verse is a series of iambic pentameters. A pentameter is a five-stress line. An iamb is a unit of poetry (called a foot) which consists of an unstressed followed by a stressed syllable. Lines which end with punctuation are called 'end-stopped'. Carrying the sense into the next line is called 'enjambement'. A series of end-stopped lines would sound very mechanical.

Ask students to explore Shakespeare's blank verse by analysing the first ten lines of Act 1, Sc VII in the following way:

- Mark the stressed syllables in each line with.
- Mark the unstressed syllable with U.
- Tick the lines which follow the iambic pentameter pattern exactly.
- Underline punctuation at the end of lines.

Students will see that Shakespeare's use of blank verse is very flexible, both in terms of slight variations to the basic pattern of the iambic pentameter and extensive use of enjambement.

Introduction:

Re-read Act I, Sc. III, Act I, Sc. VII and Act IV Sc. I. If time is limited, omit the last scene.

Development:

Shared reading of resource 25, Fate, in groups of 2–3 followed by discussion of the questions at the bottom of the page.

Plenary:

Go over the discussion questions.

Some critics believe that the witches are figments of Macbeth's imagination. However, this is probably a result of reading modern attitudes into the play. In Shakespeare's time, witches and witchcraft were believed to be real. The key question is: Did the witches *predict* Macbeth's future (a future which already existed) or did they *create* his future (either by suggestion or by magic). It is interesting to read the witches' speeches just before they meet Macbeth. This shows them actively creating mischief in the world, and suggests that they might have actively created mischief for Macbeth rather than merely being passive fortune tellers.

There are several points in the play when Macbeth almost turns away from murder. The most important is when he says to Lady Macbeth after a prolonged examination of his conscience: 'We will proceed no further in this business . . .' (see all of Act I, Sc. VII to appreciate this statement in context).

Thus we see that there are three influences on Macbeth's fate: his own ambitious personality, the three witches and Lady Macbeth. Had any one of these influences been missing, the murder would probably not have taken place.

Homework:

Write an essay about fate and free will in Macbeth using the discussion questions as a starting point for an essay plan.

Follow-up:

Students can further explore beliefs about fate at: http://www.philosophy-irc.com/fate.html Note that this site contains a philosophical discussion at a high level which makes reference to ancient Greek philosophy and theatre.

25. Fate

Fate is the belief that all events are planned out in advance. In Greek and Roman mythology, the Fates were three goddesses who allotted to each person a share of good and evil when they were born. Belief in fate is a part of many cultures today, for example in Hindu and Muslim religions. Even in modern scientific societies, many people have a lingering belief in fate, for example in astrology (see below).

A belief in fate is a necessary precondition to a belief in fortune-telling. If the future already exists, it may be possible to glimpse it in some way. Some people may have actually done this. The most famous is Nostradamus, a sixteenth century prophet who made uncannily accurate predictions about Napoleon, Hitler and a giant meteor falling on New York – an event which is still in the future. Another example is the novel *Futility* written by Morgan Robertson. This novel describes an 'unsinkable' liner which sinks by colliding with an iceberg while crossing to America. It was published thirteen years before the *Titanic* sank.

The modern scientific view is that everything happens by cause and effect. This is the exact opposite of a belief in fate. The future cannot be planned out in advance (or seen by fortune-tellers) because it simply does not exist. It depends on the outcomes of billions of complex events occurring at this moment (which the chaos theory is an attempt to describe). In this world view, each individual has the free will to make life what they want it to be.

However, it could be that both of these extreme views are wrong. We certainly do not have complete free will. Indeed, modern science has shown us that a great deal of who we are and what we do is predetermined by our genetic make-up. There is a 'middle of the road' view which is called determinism. Determinism accepts that the world works by cause and effect, but that one event is very likely to lead to another. This is the view, not only of the modern geneticist, but of the traditional astrologer.

The astrologer's birth chart is primarily a description of personality which is created by the influence of the planets. As a result of that personality, certain things are likely to happen to a person, and the planets continue to exert an external influence. Thus, many possible 'futures' exist, but the individual can exercise a degree of free will and make the best of his or her chances in life, or the worst.

DISCUSSION:

- Which of the above beliefs does Shakespeare present in *Macbeth*?

- Do you think the witches predicted Macbeth's future or caused it?

- If you think they caused it, did they cause it through their spells, or by placing a suggestion in Macbeth's mind?

- Are there any points when Macbeth tries to exercise his free will to escape from the fate told to him by the witches?

Holinshed's *Chronicles of Scotland*

Unit 3: Lesson 7

70 minutes approx.

Objectives

Sentence: Sn11 investigate ways English has changed over time and identify current trends of language change.

Reading: Rd2 synthesise information from a range of sources, shaping material to meet the reader's needs.

Writing: Wr16 present a balanced analysis of a situation, text, issue or set of ideas, taking into account a range of evidence and opinions.

Speaking and Listening: S&L9 discuss and evaluate conflicting evidence to arrive at a considered viewpoint.

Word/Sentence Activity:

Ask students to investigate Elizabethan English by studying the first extract on resource 26, Holinshed's *Chronicles Of Scotland,* which has been printed with the original spelling.

Notes: There are several differences in spelling, notably the use of ie instead of y, u instead of v, and more extensive use of final e, e.g. 'vertue', 'capteine'. Sentences are longer – sometimes to the point of confusion! 'Duncans reigne' is spelled without an apostrophe.

Overall, Holinshed is easier to understand than Shakespeare, and this is because he writes in prose.

Introduction:

Explain to students that Holinshed's *Chronicles Of Scotland* is the main source which Shakespeare used for the play. He may also have used other sources such as other histories and ballads (see Lesson 8, The Ballad O' Mackbeth).

The main reason for studying Shakespeare's sources is to find out about the changes that he made. These changes help us to understand what he was trying to achieve in his play.

Resource 26, Holinshed's *Chronicles Of Scotland,* focuses on three of the most important changes made by Shakespeare. The Arden edition (ISBN 0416101607) lists twelve changes in total (see pp. xxxiii–xl).

Shared reading of resource 26, Holinshed's *Chronicles Of Scotland.*

Development:

Students discuss the questions at the bottom of the sheet and make notes on their discussion.

Plenary:

Go over the discussion questions. Notes: Shakespeare describes Duncan as a good king (indeed, he is the ideal of kingship). He does this to make Macbeth's crime seem even more horrible. In Holinshed's Chronicle, Macbeth has an acceptable motive for his crime, i.e. he was cheated of his rightful succession to the kingship according to the law of Scotland. Shakespeare omits Macbeth's ten years of just rule as this would contradict the way the character has been developed, and delay the conclusion of the play.

Homework:

Students use the discussion notes to write the following essay:
What would the play have lost if Shakespeare had followed his source more closely?

Follow-up:

The 'Shakespeare Alive' teaching materials contain a detailed analysis of Shakespeare's use of sources. These can be found at: http://www.allshakespeare.com/plays/macbeth/sn.shtml

26. Holinshed's *Chronicles of Scotland*

A ... Makbeth, a valiant gentleman, and one that if he had not beene somewhat cruell of nature, might haue beene thought most woorthie the gouernment of a realme. On the other part, Duncane was so soft and gentle of nature, that the people wished the inclinations and maners of these two cousins to haue been so tempered and interchangeablie bestowed betwixt them, that where one had too much of clemencie, and the other of crueltie, the mean virtue betwixt these two extremities might haue reigned by indifferent partition in them both, so should Duncane haue prooued a woorthie king, and Makbeth an excellent capteine. The beginning of Duncans reigne was verie quiet and peaceable, with anie notable trouble; but after it was perceiued how negligent he was in punishing offendors, manie misruled persons took occasion thereof to trouble the peace and quiet state of the common-wealth, by seditious commotions which first had their beginnings in this wise ...

B ... it chanced that king Duncan having two sons by his wife which was the daughter of Siward Earl of Northumberland, he made the elder of the sons called Malcolm Prince of Cumberland, as it were thereby to appoint him his successor in the kingdom, immediately after his decease. Macbeth sore troubled herewith, for that he saw by this his hope sore hindered (where, by the old lawes of the realme, the ordinance was, that if he should succeed were not of able age to take the charge upon himself, he that was next of blood unto him should be admitted) he began to take council how he might usurp the kingdom by force, having a just quarrel to do (as he took the matter) for that Duncan did what in him lay to defraud hiim of all manner of title and claim, which he might in time to come, pretend unto the crown ...

C ... Macbeth ... governed the realme for the space of ten years in equal justice. But this was a counterfeit zeal of equity showed by him, partly against his natural inclination to purchase thereby the favour of the people. Shortly after, he began to show what he was, instead of equity practising cruelty. For the prick of conscience (as it chanceth ever in tyrants, and such as attain to any estate by unrighteous means) caused him ever to fear, lest he be served of the same cup, as he had ministered to his predecessor.

DISCUSSION:

⬤ Read extract A. What is the difference between the character of Duncan in this extract, compared to his character in the play? Why do you think Shakespeare changed his character?

⬤ Read extract B. What do we learn from this extract about the way in which Duncan arranged for his successor? How does this change our view of Macbeth? Why do you think Shakespeare omitted this information?

⬤ Read extract C. How does this account of Macbeth's reign differ from Shakespeare's? Why was it necessary for Shakespeare to change this?

The Ballad O' Mackbeth

Unit 3: Lesson 8

70 minutes approx.

Objectives

Sentence: Sn10 explore differing attitudes to language and identify characteristics of standard English that make it the dominant mode of public communication – *by comparing it with a dialect.*

Reading: Rd7 compare the presentation of ideas, values or emotions in related or contrasting texts.

Speaking and Listening: S&L7 identify the underlying themes, implications and issues raised by a talk, reading or programme.

Starter Activity:

Explain to students that the Scots language is Gaelic (or Gallic), a language which is still spoken in the north of Scotland. The Scots dialect is a version of English which developed from the Northumbrian dialect of Anglo-Saxon. Ask students to spend ten minutes looking through the ballad to find the differences between Standard English and Scots dialect.

STANDARD ENGLISH	SCOTS DIALECT
child	bairn
dagger	dirk
eyes	e'en (note archaic 'en' plural)
long 'o', e.g. 'home'	long 'a', e.g. 'hame'
etc.	

Introduction:

Explain to students that 'The Ballad O' Mackbeth' is an anonymous border ballad (which has been slightly abridged by omitting a few verses from the beginning and end, and some descriptive verses from the middle). It is tempting to think that it is the ballad mentioned by Kempe in his 'Nine Days Wonder' (1600) which could have been one of Shakespeare's sources. However, the language and style of the ballad suggest a later date, and the story is not detailed enough to be of much use as a source. The reference to the witches in the ballad is evidence that the ballad was written after the play (and is perhaps based on it), as Shakespeare seems to have got the idea of the witches from another story about a conspiracy against King Duff.

The ballad is a useful revision tool as it provides a summary of the play in a more interesting and memorable format than the usual prose summary. It is therefore recommended that this lesson is not used immediately after the previous sequence of lessons, but at a later date for revision purposes.

The ballad can be used as it is, or presented in the form of a sequencing excise (see 'Development' below). The following glossary may be helpful:

ane	own
e'en	eyes
blude	blood
dane	down
dirk	dagger
evermair	evermore
gane	gone
hame	home

mun	must
sair	sore
vexed	angered
wuid	would

Development:

The ballad is printed on the resource sheet in its correct sequence, but after copying, it could be cut up and placed in an envelope (one copy for each pair of students). The envelopes are then given to students who work in pairs on the following activities:

- Re-sequence the ballad.

- Taking verses in turn, match the verses to scenes in the play. Write line numbers from the text by the side of each verse, and read the scenes aloud.

- Several minor incidents are not described in the ballad. Make a list of these (see follow-up).

Plenary:

Discuss the similarities and differences between the ballad and the play.

The ballad is much shorter (less than 450 words). It tells the story with breathless haste, rarely pausing to develop description of place or character, or to explore the issues. Several events are left out, e.g. the murder of Macduff's wife and children, Lady Macbeth's madness, or the way Macbeth rules Scotland. The ballad thus falls into the category of 'verse chronicle', i.e. a type of popular history told in verse, rather than literature.

Discuss what the ballad has helped students to remember about the play. As well as reminding students of the basic plot, it should also remind them of the importance of background details, and detailed character description, particularly motives such as ambition and feelings such as guilt and remorse.

Homework:

Give each student a fresh copy of the resource sheets on A3-sized paper and ask them to write in the right-hand column a PROSE summary of the story of *Macbeth* which, as far as possible, parallels the stages of the story in the ballad. Remind them to spell all names as they are spelled in the play! If A3 is not available, another A4 sheet can be pasted to the right of the ballad sheet. Explain to students that if they rewrite each ballad verse in simple modern English, and add the most important of the missing incidents, they will have a good summary of the play.

Follow-up:

Some students may enjoy writing extra verses about these minor incidents and adding them to the ballad.

For a somewhat more substantial verse chronicle (which also includes an account of *Macbeth*), see William Stewart's *Buik of the Chroniclis of Scotland* (1531–5).

27. The Ballad O' Mackbeth

Mackbeth an' Banquho ganging hame
Were hailed by witches three:
'Mackbeth, o' Cawdor thou art thegn,
An' king thou suin shalt be.'

To Banquho too they prophesied
Saying he ne'er wuid get
The kingship fur himsel' although
A king's line wuid beget.

An' when Rosse told Mackbeth the news
That he wa' thegn o' Cawder
He thought him that he mun be king,
E'en if 'twa' by murder.

Sae when King Duncane made his son,
Malcolme, the country's heir,
An' Prince o' Cumberland the while,
Mackbeth wa' vexéd sair.

News that the king wuid bide the night
Wa' sent to Mackbeth's wife
In Inverness. 'Twas then she vowed
That they wuid tak' his life.

When Duncane an' Mackbeth arrived
Mackbeth's resolve wa' gane,
But she said, 'If thou art afeared,
I'll kill him on my ain.'

The clock struck midnight as Mackbeth
Crept into Duncane's room
An' plunged a dirk into his breast
An' sent him to his doom.

Mackduffe an' Lennox then appeared
Asking to see the king.
Sae Mackbeth took them to his room
An' watched as they went in.

'The King is murthered!' Mackduffe cried,
'Wi' blude the guards are red!'
'Alas that here,' said Lady Mackbeth,
'Our king should be found dead!'

The sun that day wa' hid by cloud
An' monstrous sights were seen:
Horses eating their own flesh
An' babes born wi'out e'en.

Malcolme an' Donald Bane in fear
To England then went doun,
An' wi' them safely oot o' the way
Mackbeth could claim the crown.

At Forres Castéll Mackbeth reigned
But couldna reign in peace
For fear o' Banquho an' his kin;
Fro' them he sought release.

He sent hired murtherers tae kill
Banquho an' his son.
Banquho they killed wi' wicked dirks
But Fleance still lived on.

That night, his hair aw streaked wi' blude,
The ghost o' Banquho came
Tae Mackbeth's feast. What could he do
But sent his guests straight hame?

Then tae the witches Mackbeth went
Tae ask what lay ahead.
'Double, double, toil an' trouble –
Beware Mackduffe,' they said.

'None o' woman borne can harm,
Mackbeth, an' thou shalt reign
As Scotland's king 'til Birnam Wood
Do come tae Dunsinane.'

An' then came Banquho's ghost again
Showing his royal heir,
An' others coming after him
It seemed for evermair.

Mackduffe tae Northumberland flew,
Leaving his bairns an' wife,
There tae join Siward an' Malcolme's men
Tae fight Mackbeth at Fife.

Battle began at Birnam Wood
Which Malcolme's men cut dane
Tae use as a disguise while they
Did march tae Dunsinane.

An' then Mackduffe attacked Mackbeth
'No mon o' woman born
Fear I!' said he. Replied Mackduffe,
'Frae the womb wa' I torn!'

Mackduffe at last dispatched Mackbeth
Wi' an almighty swing.
The battle o'er, the folk rejoiced,
An' Malcolme wa' crowned King.
Anonymous border ballad

(slightly simplified and abridged)

UNIT 4: CRIME AND PUNISHMENT

Title of unit: CRIME AND PUNISHMENT

Resources
Book: *The Hound of the Baskervilles*, by Sir Arthur Conan Doyle.
CD: *Martin Guerre*. The Boublil and Schönberg Musical, 4th Version (UK/US Tours) – November 1998–present (optional)

Year: 9	Term: 2, second half	Duration: 10 lessons	Set: All

NLS objectives		NC objectives
Sherlock Holmes	Rd12, Wr9	En2 8a) iii) works of fiction by two major writers published before 1914 – Sir Arthur Conan Doyle.
Baskerville Hall	Sn2, Rd9	
The Hound of the Baskervilles	Wd6, Rd18, Wr17	En2 8c) drama . . . by major writers from different cultures and traditions – Sir Arthur Conan Doyle (adapted).
A Detective Story	Wd6, Rd12, Wr14	
Solve it Yourself	Rd14, S&L15	En2 9b) print-based information and reference texts.
The Speckled Band	Rd14, S&L15	
Martin Guerre, Part 1	Rd6, Wr16, S&L9	En2 9c) media and moving-image texts (musical).
Martin Guerre, Part 2	Rd6, Wr16	
Martin Guerre – the Musical	Rd8, Wr16	En3 1a) draw on their experience of good fiction . . . watching and performing plays.
Detective Story Cards	Wd: various, Sn: various, S&L9	

Teaching sequence	Outcomes
Week 1: Sherlock Holmes Baskerville Hall	Write a character sketch of Sherlock Holmes. *Write an analysis of the description of Baskerville Hall.
Week 2: *The Hound of the Baskervilles* A Detective Story	Write about suspense in Chapter 14. *The Hound of the Baskervilles* as a detective story.
Week 3: Solve it Yourself *The Speckled Band*	Write in the style of the author. *Write an ending for the play.
Week 4: Martin Guerre, Part 1 Martin Guerre, Part 2	*Write a speech for the defence or the prosecution. Write Bertrand's secret diary.
Week 5: Martin Guerre – the Musical Detective Story Cards	Write a review of the musical.
	Assessment pieces

Sherlock Holmes

Unit 4: Lesson 1

70 minutes approx.

Objectives

Sentence: (not listed) write a summary of a text in a specified number of words.

Reading: Rd12 analyse and discuss the use made of rhetorical devices in a text.

Writing: Wr9 integrate diverse information into a coherent and comprehensive account.

Word/Sentence Activity:

Using resource 28, Summary, revise the key skills necessary to write a good summary.

Introduction:

Begin by brainstorming students' prior knowledge about Sherlock Holmes.

Shared reading of Chapter 1.

Students discuss what can be learned about the character of Sherlock Holmes and his methods of deduction; and about his relationship with Dr Watson.

Development:

Shared reading of Chapters 2 and 3.

Students write a 100 word summary of the facts of the case.

Plenary:

Discuss the case and how Holmes might use his special methods of detection to solve it.

Homework:

Write a character sketch of Sherlock Holmes. This can include background information from the brainstorming session as well as specific information from the shared reading.

Follow-up:

Student can find out more about Sherlock Holmes at:

http://holmes-sherlock.com/links/link131.html

Another valuable site is: http://www.sherlock-holmes.org/english.htm. This includes the complete Sherlock Holmes canon online.

28. Summary

A *summary* is a shortened version of a text which has been written to include the main points. It is different from an *abridgement* which is a shorter version of a text created by omitting phrases, sentences and sometimes whole paragraphs from the original.

STAGE 1 – SELECTING KEY INFORMATION

- Highlight or underline the most important points (tip: look for the topic sentences of each paragraph as a starting point).

- Count the number of words you have highlighted.

- If you need more words, highlight some additional points. If you need fewer words, delete the least important points from those you have highlighted.

- Resist the temptation to add additional information or your own opinions.

STAGE 2 – REPHRASING THE INFORMATION

The final summary will usually consist of ONE paragraph. To create this paragraph you will need to rewrite your highlighted text so that it reads well, for example by:

- expressing two or more key points in single sentences

- using pronouns where necessary to avoid clumsy repetition

- rewording difficult phraseology into your own words.

TASK 1:

Summarise a text that you are working on at the moment, e.g. summarise a short information text to 25 per cent of its original length.

TASK 2:

Experiment with the *abridgement* of part of a novel to make it more suitable for a younger audience – remember, in an abridgement you are only allowed to *cut* words, phrases and paragraphs, not *reword* them.

TASK 3:

Experiment with the *autosummarise* feature available in some word-processors. Summarise a text to different percentages of the original and see how well the feature works. Try to find out how autosummarise programs work.

Baskerville Hall

Unit 4: Lesson 2

70 minutes approx.

Objectives

Sentence: Sn2 use the full range of punctuation to clarify and emphasise meaning for a reader.

Reading: Rd9 compare themes and styles of two writers from different times.

Word/Sentence Activity:

Revise the following terms to describe sentences: *simple, compound* and *complex*.

Simple: a simple sentence contains one clause.
Compound: a compound sentence contains two or more clauses of equal weight linked by the coordinating conjunctions 'and' or 'but'.
Complex: a complex sentence contains a main clause and one or more subordinate clauses which can be linked in a number of ways, e.g. by subordinating conjunctions, relative pronouns, etc.
Compound-complex: sentences which are a combination of both of the above.

Introduction:

Shared reading of Chapter 6.

Development:

This masterly description of Baskerville Hall and its setting is very important in building up the atmosphere of fear and suspense. Ask students, working in pairs, to analyse the description by working through the tasks on resource 29, 'Baskerville Hall'. Less able students could be asked to look for linking words (conjunctions) only.

Plenary:

Discuss the tasks on resource 29, Baskerville Hall. Detailed notes on Task 3 are given below. Explain to students that the main purpose of this exercise is to demonstrate how various grammatical techniques can be used to build interesting and varied sentences:

Sentence 1: a compound sentence consisting of two clauses linked by 'and'.
Sentence 2: a simple sentence extended with a phrase in apposition.
Sentence 3: a complex sentence in which a subordinate clause is linked to the main clause by the conjunction 'for'.
Sentence 4: a compound-complex sentence in which the two main clauses are linked by 'but' and the second clause is modified by a subordinate clause linked by the relative pronoun 'who', and further extended by another clause linked by 'and'.
Sentence 5: a compound sentence consisting of two clauses linked by 'and', the first of which is extended by a phrase in apposition.
Sentence 6: a compound sentence with three clauses linked by 'and' and 'but', the last of which is extended by two phrases in apposition.

Homework:

Students write an essay entitled 'The Description of Baskerville Hall'. They can use the tasks as a template for an essay. Encourage them to support their points with quotations from the text.

Follow-up:

Students could write their own description of a place using Doyle's description as a model (this could perhaps be used later on as a setting for their own crime story).

29. Baskerville Hall

Re-read Chapter 6, then work through the following tasks with a partner:

1. Pick out words and phrases which emphasise the wildness of the moor around Baskerville Hall.

2. What effect does the presence of the escaped convict have on the mood and atmosphere of the description?

3. Re-read the paragraph beginning 'The train pulled up at a small wayside station . . .' and state whether each sentence is simple, compound, complex or compound-complex, and comment on how the clauses are joined.

4. Pick out the adjectives and figures of speech that are used to describe Baskerville Hall.

5. Pick out the descriptive details that help the reader to imagine Baskerville Hall.

6. What is the overall effect of these descriptive techniques?

7. What effect do the last two paragraphs have on the reader?

8. In the box below, sketch your impression of Baskerville Hall.

The Hound of the Baskervilles

Unit 4: Lesson 3

70 minutes approx.

Objectives

Word: Wd6 know and use the terms that are useful for analysing language, e.g., *pronouns*.

Reading: Rd18 discuss a substantial prose text, sharing perceptions, negotiating common readings and accounting for differences of view.

Writing: Wr17 cite specific and relevant textual evidence to justify critical judgements about texts.

Word/Sentence Activity:

Use resource 30, 'Pronouns' to revise the different types of pronouns. Less able students should concentrate on personal and possessive pronouns only.

Introduction:

Shared reading of Chapter 14.

Using four different colours, highlight examples of the different types of pronouns on the first page of Chapter 14. Note: for this and the following activity, it would be preferable for students to work with photocopies of this chapter rather than to write in the actual texts.

Development:

Ask students, working in pairs, to trace the build-up of suspense in this chapter. A good way to do this is to highlight or underline each point at which the suspense is increased.

Plenary:

Discuss how the suspense is built up:

The suspense begins with the first paragraph which states 'the great ordeal was before us'. The danger of the plan is emphasised by Holmes's question to Lestrade: 'Are you armed?' The fog introduces a strong element of suspense – will Sir Henry leave the Stapletones before the fog closes in? Holmes comments: 'If he isn't out in a quarter of an hour the path will be covered.' They hear the sound of Sir Henry's 'quick steps' and moments after Holmes cries: 'Look out! It's coming!' At this point the suspense is at its height – will the hound kill Sir Henry before Holmes can kill the hound? When the hound appears, it is so terrifying that Lestrade throws himself on the ground in terror. Holmes and Watson fire their pistols and the hound howls. They realise that 'If he was vulnerable, he was mortal' – the suspense eases slightly. They race to Sir Henry and shoot the hound dead just in time. Holmes realises that its supernatural appearance is created by phosphorus. The story is now over. All that remains is to tidy up the loose ends, and in the last chapter, to give a full explanation of what happened.

Homework:

Ask students to write an explanation of how suspense is built up in this chapter. Encourage them to quote examples from the text as evidence for each main point.

Follow-up:

Compare this scene with a film or TV version to see how the director builds up suspense using the visual medium and additional effects such as music.

30. Pronouns

Pronouns are used to avoid unnecessary repetition and to show how clauses are related. There are several types of pronouns, the main ones are listed below:

PERSONAL PRONOUNS

Personal pronouns are used for people or things –
(subject) I, you, he, she, it, we, they;
(object) me, him, her, it, us, them.

EXAMPLE

The teacher frowned at Sally. *She* handed *him* the missing homework. (Note 'she' is the subject of the sentence and is therefore a subject pronoun; 'him' is the object of the sentence and is therefore an object pronoun).

POSSESSIVE PRONOUNS

Possessive pronouns show ownership –
mine, yours, his, hers, ours, theirs.

DEMONSTRATIVE PRONOUNS

Demonstrative pronouns point things out –
this, that, these, those.

EXAMPLE OF BOTH OF THE ABOVE

That calculator is *mine*.

According to Collins Cobuild English Grammar (1.110 – 1.113) 'mine' is a possessive pronoun and 'that' is a demonstrative pronoun (1.123 – 1.125). Crystal (Rediscover Grammar, p. 133) also classifies it as a demonstrative pronoun. However, it appears that some older grammars do classify 'that' as a demonstrative adjective.

RELATIVE PRONOUNS

Relative pronouns refer to somebody or something that has been mentioned before *and at the same* time join clauses together –
who, whom, which, that.

EXAMPLE

That is the pupil *who* got top marks in the maths test.

TASK 1:

Write another example to show the use of each kind of pronoun.

TASK 2:

Find examples of the different types of pronouns in a text you are reading.

A Detective Story

Unit 4: Lesson 4

70 minutes approx.

Objectives

Word: Wd6 know and use the terms that are useful for analysing language, e.g., *connectives*.

Reading: Rd12 analyse and discuss the use made of rhetorical devices in a text.

Writing: Wr14 make a counter-argument to a view that has been expressed, addressing weaknesses in the argument and offering alternatives.

Word/Sentence Activity:

Using resource 31, 'Connectives', revise connectives.

Introduction:

Shared reading of Chapter 15.

Ask students, working in pairs, to find examples of connectives in the first two pages of the chapter.

Development:

Discuss detective fiction genre by asking students to brainstorm other detective characters both old and new, e.g. Brother Cadfael, Poirot, Inspector Morse, Taggart, Daziel and Pascoe. What features do the characters and the stories have in common?

Give out resource 32, *The Hound of The Baskervilles* as a Detective Story, and ask students to see how far the points in the left-hand column agree with the common features they identified in discussion. Note that the points should be modified as necessary so that it is a true reflection of their analysis of the detective story genre.

The next step is for students to write notes in the right-hand column showing how far *The Hound of the Baskervilles* fulfils the criteria for the genre.

Plenary:

Discuss how far *The Hound of the Baskervilles* fulfils the criteria for the detective story genre. Note: students will find that it is an almost perfect example of the genre, and this is partly because the Sherlock Holmes stories were one of the main influences in developing it!

Homework:

Students use the categories on resource 32, *The Hound of The Baskervilles* as a Detective Story as the basic structure for an essay on the novel. Essays should be developed with information from previous lessons, for example, an analysis of the character of Sherlock Holmes, an analysis of the creation of atmosphere particularly in the description of Baskerville Hall, and an analysis of how Doyle builds up suspense.

Follow-up:

There have been many film and TV versions of this story which would be worth studying, for example: *The Hound Of The Baskervilles*, 1939, director, Sidney Lanfield, starring Basil Rathbone and *The Hound Of The Baskervilles*, 1959, Hammer Films, director, Terence Fisher, starring Peter Cushing.

31. Connectives

Connectives are used to link ideas together (note that they are sometimes called adjuncts).

ADDING ANOTHER POINT

also

furthermore

besides

moreover

as well

too

at the same time

further

GIVING A DIFFERENT POINT OF VIEW

nonetheless

on the other hand

alternatively

by contrast

however

on the contrary

instead

still

then again

yet

conversely

nevertheless

even so

though

DRAWING A CONCLUSION FROM A FACT OR FACTS

so

hence

as a result

thereby

therefore

thus

consequently

accordingly

TO ORGANISING POINTS IN AN ESSAY

to sum up

secondly

in conclusion

first

lastly

then

thirdly

finally

TASK 1:

Find examples of connectives in a text you are reading.

TASK 2:

Keep this table beside you the next time you write an essay and use it to help you to link your ideas more effectively.

32. *The Hound of the Baskervilles* as a Detective Story

SOME FEATURES OF DETECTIVE STORIES	THE HOUND OF THE BASKERVILLES
An interesting and unusual main character with particular techniques of investigation.	
An interesting setting.	
A crime which is a real challenge to solve.	
Clues which the reader can use to try to solve the crime him/herself.	
One or more 'red herrings' (a red herring is something which distracts the reader's attention from the real villain).	
Some unexpected twists in the plot.	
Exciting scenes in which the detective faces danger.	
A final explanation of all the details of the crime.	

Solve it Yourself

Unit 4: Lesson 5

70 minutes approx.

Objectives

Reading: Rd14 analyse the language, form and dramatic impact of scenes and plays by published dramatists.

Writing: (not listed) write a continuation in the style of the author.

Speaking and Listening: S&L15 write critical evaluations of performances they have seen or in which they have participated, identifying the contributions of the writer, director and actors.

Starter Activity:

Students read a sample of the original text from *The Adventure of the Speckled Band* and discuss how it could be dramatised (adapted for stage).

Introduction:

Students work in groups of 4–5. Allocate parts for each person (Sherlock Holmes and Miss Stoner are the largest parts. The two smaller parts can be played by one student). Students should then read through the whole play to get to know the plot and the characters.

Students discuss the differences between the original text and this dramatisation.

Development:

Students now try to solve the mystery. The clues are clearly pointed out by Holmes throughout the play and some helpful prompts are provided at the end of the script. While students are working on their solution, the teacher should move from group to group giving help by guiding students' thinking, and giving helpful hints where appropriate.

Plenary:

The whole class discusses ideas about the solution. Note that it is unlikely that any students will be able to guess the solution as it is quite complicated – though some may get parts of it. The full solution is as follows:

> Dr Stoner would lose half his income if his stepdaughters married. Therefore, when Julia gets engaged he plans to kill her. He does this by training a poisonous snake (remember his hobby of collecting Indian animals) which he keeps in a safe and feeds on milk. When he whistles the snake crawls through the false air vent and down the false bell rope (which he had put in for the purpose) and on to Julia's bed. When he whistles again, the snake returns. He plans to do the same to Helen that very night.

Homework:

Ask students to rewrite the playscript in story form continuing from the original opening on resource 33, 'The Adventure of the Speckled Band'.

Follow-up:

Sir Arthur Conan Doyle's actual ending could be read out to the class. The story continues on page 142 of *The Adventures of Sherlock Holmes*, A. Conan Doyle, Moby Books, ISBN 0–7105–0322 – or students could read the whole story themselves online at: http://www.sherlock-holmes.org/english.htm

33. *The Adventure of the Speckled Band*

On glancing over my notes of the seventy odd cases in which I have during the last eight years studied the methods of my friend Sherlock Holmes, I find many tragic, some comic, a large number merely strange, but none commonplace; for, working as he did rather for the love of his art than for the acquirement of wealth, he refused to associate himself with any investigation which did not tend towards the unusual, and even the fantastic. Of all these varied cases, however, I cannot recall any which presented more singular features than that which was associated with the well-known Surrey family of the Roylotts of Stoke Moran. The events in question occurred in the early days of my association with Holmes, when we were sharing rooms as bachelors in Baker Street. It is possible that I might have placed them upon record before, but a promise of secrecy was made at the time, from which I have only been freed during the last month by the untimely death of the lady to whom the pledge was given. It is perhaps as well that the facts should now come to light, for I have reasons to know that there are widespread rumours as to the death of Dr Grimesby Roylott which tend to make the matter even more terrible than the truth.

It was early in April in the year '83 that I woke one morning to find Sherlock Holmes standing, fully dressed, by the side of my bed. He was a late riser, as a rule, and as the clock on the mantelpiece showed me that it was only a quarter-past seven, I blinked up at him in some surprise, and perhaps just a little resentment, for I was myself regular in my habits.

'Very sorry to knock you up, Watson,' said he, 'but it's the common lot this morning. Mrs. Hudson has been knocked up, she retorted upon me, and I on you.'

'What is it, then – a fire?'

'No; a client. It seems that a young lady has arrived in a considerable state of excitement, who insists upon seeing me. She is waiting now in the sitting-room. Now, when young ladies wander about the metropolis at this hour of the morning, and knock sleepy people up out of their beds, I presume that it is something very pressing which they have to communicate. Should it prove to be an interesting case, you would, I am sure, wish to follow it from the outset. I thought, at any rate, that I should call you and give you the chance.'

'My dear fellow, I would not miss it for anything.'

I had no keener pleasure than in following Holmes in his professional investigations, and in admiring the rapid deductions, as swift as intuitions, and yet always founded on a logical basis, with which he unravelled the problems which were submitted to him. I rapidly threw on my clothes and was ready in a few minutes to accompany my friend down to the sitting-room. A lady dressed in black and heavily veiled, who had been sitting in the window, rose as we entered.

Sir Arthur Conan Doyle, 1892

34. The Speckled Band

by Sir Arthur Conan Doyle, dramatised version

CAST

SHERLOCK HOLMES

DR WATSON

MISS HELEN STONER

HOUSEKEEPER

DR ROYLOTT

(the last two can be played by one pupil)

SCENE 1

Inside Sherlock Holmes' bachelor apartment at 221B Baker Street. The time is 8.15 A.M.

HOUSEKEEPER: *(Knocking and putting her head round the door)* There's a young woman to see you, sir.

HOLMES: What! At this early hour! Very well, show her in.

HOUSEKEEPER: Yes, sir.

HOLMES: *(Calling)* Watson!

WATSON: *(From off stage)* Coming, Holmes.

HOLMES: *(As Watson enters)* A new case, I think. Would you like to be in on it?

WATSON: I wouldn't miss it for anything. My greatest pleasure is admiring your powers of deduction!

HOLMES: Then you shall assist me! Take out your notepad and make notes as I direct!

HOUSEKEEPER: *(Knocking and showing Miss Stoner in)* Miss Helen Stoner, sir.

HOLMES: *(Standing and showing Miss Stoner to a chair)* Please sit down, Miss Stoner.

MISS STONER: Thank you, Mr Holmes.

HOLMES: Well, Miss Stoner, what can I do for you?

MISS STONER: Mr Holmes, I have come to you for help.

HOLMES: Then tell me everything you can. Begin at the beginning, and take your time.

MISS STONER: I live with my stepfather, Dr Grimesby Roylott. He was a doctor in Calcutta, India, when he met my mother, Mrs Stoner, who was the widow of an army officer. She was killed in a railway accident and we moved back to Stoke Moran in England. My mother left over £1,000* in her will, but the will stated that when my sister and I married, £250 must go to each of us.

WATSON: Were you happy in your new home?

MISS STONER: Alas, no! My stepfather shut himself up in the old house and showed no interest in anything except his strange hobbies.

HOLMES: Indeed! What are they?

MISS STONER: He has a passion for Indian animals and keeps a cheetah and a baboon as pets. He is also fond of gypsies. He lets them camp in his grounds, and in return, they let him travel with them, sometimes for weeks at a time.

HOLMES: *(To Dr Watson)* That could be our first CLUE, Watson. Make a note of his hobbies.

MRS STONER: Then, two years ago, my sister died.

WATSON: How did she die?

*Worth about £100,000 in today's money.

MISS STONER: Strangely, I fear. One Christmas, Julia got engaged to a naval officer. I thought my father would object, but he said nothing. Then, two weeks before her wedding, a terrible thing happened.

HOLMES: Give me the exact details.

MISS STONER: The house is very old and the bedrooms are on the ground floor. The first is Dr Roylott's, the second my sister's and the third my own. There are no doors connecting them, but they all open into the same corridor. We always lock our doors at night because of the cheetah and baboon.

HOLMES: And the windows of these rooms?

MISS STONER: They face a large lawn. That night Dr Roylott had gone to his room early. I heard a low whistle, and thought it must be the gipsies. Then I heard a wild scream. It was my sister's voice. I rushed into the corridor. As I did so I heard another low whistle, and a few moments later I heard a clanging sound, as if some heavy metal had fallen. I ran to my sister's door and found it open, with Julia clinging to it. She shrieked in pain: 'Oh God! Helen! It was the band! The speckled band!' Then she died.

HOLMES: Watson, here are more CLUES. Make a note of the whistle, the clanging sound and the speckled band – especially the speckled band!

WATSON: (Writing) Did the police investigate?

MISS STONER: They were very thorough. Julia's door had been locked from the inside, and her windows had bars and shutters. The chimney was bricked up. They said it was certain that she was alone when she died.

HOLMES: Were there any marks of violence on her?

MISS STONER: No, nothing.

WATSON: Any signs of poison?

MISS STONER: None.

HOLMES: Two more CLUES. Note them, Watson.

WATSON: (Writing) What do you think she died of?

MISS STONER: Fear – a terrifying shock.

WATSON: Were gypsies camped in the grounds at the time?

MISS STONER: Yes.

HOLMES: What do you think she meant by the speckled band?

MISS STONER: (Uncertainly) Perhaps she was referring to the spotted handkerchiefs the gypsies wear on their heads.

HOLMES: (Shaking his head) I'm not satisfied. There is more to it than that. She would not die of fear from seeing a gypsy, whether he was wearing a spotted handkerchief or not. However, go on with your story.

MISS STONER: About a month ago an old friend, Mr Armitage, asked me to marry him. My father did not object, but soon after he asked me to move into my sister's old room. Then, last night, I heard the strange whistle again. The whistle that came just before her death. I was frightened, and came straight to you this morning.

HOLMES: I must see your room as soon as possible. Can it be done without your stepfather knowing it?

MISS STONER: My stepfather said he would be in London all day today, and I can easily get our housekeeper out of the way.

HOLMES: Excellent! We will arrive at Stoke Moran early this afternoon.

MISS STONER: (Rising) Thank you, Mr Holmes, and you too, Dr Watson. I feel better after talking to you.

Miss Stoner exits.

WATSON: What do you make of it, Holmes?

HOLMES: A dark and sinister business.

Suddenly, the door bursts open and a huge man in a long frock coat and top hat enters, looking angry. It is Dr Roylott.

DR ROYLOTT: *(Loudly)* Which of you is Holmes?

HOLMES: *(Quietly)* I am. But who are you?

DR ROYLOTT: Dr Grimesby Roylott of Stoke Moran.

WATSON: *(Pleasantly)* Ah, a fellow doctor. Please have a seat.

DR ROYLOTT: *(Shouting)* I will do nothing of the kind. I followed my stepdaughter here. What has she been telling you?

HOLMES: *(To Watson)* My, the weather is chilly.

DR ROYLOTT: *(Screaming)* What has she been telling you?

WATSON: I think it will be milder tomorrow.

DR ROYLOTT: Ignore me will you. Well, take this as a warning!

Dr Roylott takes an iron poker from the fireplace and bends it into a curve. Then he throws it down and exits.

WATSON: He's a friendly character!

HOLMES: I'm not as big as he is, but if he had stayed, I might have shown him something!

He takes the poker from the floor and straightens it out again.

SCENE 2

Inside Stoke Moran House. Miss Stoner enters with Sherlock Holmes and Dr Watson.

MISS STONER: My stepfather won't be back before evening.

WATSON: We have already met him! He came to threaten us just after you left.

MISS STONER: Good Heavens! He must have followed me!

HOLMES: There is no time to lose. Please take us to your room so that we may examine it.

Miss Stoner takes them to her room and they look round it with great care. Holmes uses his magnifying glass to examine the hinges of the window shutters and the lock on the door.

HOLMES: No one could pass through those window shutters. The lock on the door is strong, and the chimney is bricked up.

MISS STONER: Just as I told you.

Holmes looks round again and notices something else.

HOLMES: Where does this bell pull ring?

MISS STONER: In the housekeeper's room, I suppose. It was put there a couple of years ago, just before my sister died.

Holmes decides that it looks odd. He pulls it vigorously but it makes no sound.

HOLMES: It's a dummy! It is not even attached to a wire. It goes straight through that air vent into the next room!

WATSON: Well spotted, Holmes. I didn't even notice it!

HOLMES: When was the air vent put in?

MISS STONER: At about the same time as the bell pull. Dr Roylott said the room was stuffy.

HOLMES: Why does the vent go through to the next room instead of outside?

MISS STONER: I never thought about it.

HOLMES: *(Thinking aloud)* Strange . . . bell pulls that don't ring, air vents that don't ventilate . . . Note them down as CLUES, Watson. Now, Miss Stoner, I should like to see your stepfather's bedroom.

Miss Stoner shows them into the next room. Inside there is a bed, a shelf of medical books, a wooden chair, an air vent, and a large iron safe with a saucer of milk on it. Holmes walks around examining everything carefully.

HOLMES: *(Tapping the safe)* What's in here.

MISS STONER: My stepfather's business papers.

HOLMES: Have you actually seen inside?

MISS STONER: I don't think so.

WATSON: Could there be a cat in it?

MISS STONER: *(Surprised)* What a strange idea!

WATSON: Well, what is this saucer of milk for?

MISS STONER: We don't have a cat, but my stepfather does keep a cheetah and a baboon.

WATSON: That little saucer of milk could hardly satisfy a big cheetah!

HOLMES: *(After thinking for a moment)* Then it must be for some other, smaller animal. Note it down as a CLUE, Watson. And while you are writing, note down another CLUE. *(Pointing to the wall above the safe)* There is the other side of the air vent which we saw in Miss Stoner's room.

WATSON: Is that all, Holmes?

HOLMES: Yes, Watson, I have seen enough. Miss Stoner, you must do exactly as I tell you. Your life may depend on it!

MISS STONER: I shall do whatever you tell me, Mr Holmes.

HOLMES: Your bedroom faces the inn where we are staying. When your stepfather goes to bed, put a lamp in your window and open your shutters as a signal to us. Then, perhaps, we shall find out what is causing those strange noises!

MISS STONER: Why, Mr Holmes, I believe that you already know!

HOLMES: *(With a smile)* Perhaps I do, Miss Stoner, perhaps I do.

CAN YOU SOLVE THE MYSTERY OF THE SPECKLED BAND?

- Make sure that you know the basic facts of the case.

- What motive has Dr Roylott for murdering his stepdaughters?

- Think very carefully about each clue in turn.

- Think carefully about the descriptions of the two rooms.

- What could Julia Stoner have meant by 'the speckled band?'

When you think you have solved the case, improvise an ending to the play.

The Speckled Band

Unit 4: Lesson 6

70 minutes approx.

Objectives

Reading: Rd14 analyse the language, form and dramatic impact of scenes and plays by published dramatists.

Writing: (not listed) write playscripts and/or short screenplays which explore and exploit the presentational conventions of drama and film.

Speaking and Listening: S&L15 write critical evaluations of performances they have seen or in which they have participated, identifying the contributions of the writer, director and actors.

Starter Activity:

Using the script of *The Speckled Band* as a model (resource 34), ask students to investigate the conventions of writing playscripts. They should come up with a list something like the following:

- The script begins with a cast list (in order of appearance).
- The script is divided into scenes and acts.
- Speech marks are not used.
- Stage directions are brief and are written in the present tense.
- Brief directions to actors are given in brackets at the beginning of the speech.

Introduction:

Students now act out their play. A large space is desirable. If there is no alternative but the classroom, then students should stay at their desks and present the play as a radio play. In a larger space, each group should be allocated an area which is their 'stage'. They cannot move outside this area. They should decide on which side of their stage the audience is sitting, and should play to the audience. They should now 'block' their play, i.e. plan out the moves. Scenery should be limited to a few chairs and tables plus a few simple props such as a magnifying glass for Holmes, a box for a safe, a saucer, a cord for a bell pull etc.

Development:

Each group should improvise an ending based on the plenary discussion of the previous lesson. However, they should be encouraged to adapt this freely.

Plenary:

Evaluate the performance against the following criteria:

- Presenting the scripted drama, e.g. delivery of lines, movements, etc.
- Improvised drama, e.g. improvisations true to character, etc.
- Ideas for the ending, e.g. fit the story so far, etc.

Homework:

Write the improvised ending in play script form.

Follow-up:

If time allows (e.g. another double lesson), students could present their play to an audience (e.g. another class). To avoid the monotony of watching the same play several times the teacher should choose different groups to present: Scene 1, Scene 2, and a range of different improvised endings.

Students might like to investigate whether this unusual way of committing murder would actually have worked. To do this they should investigate the habits of snakes in general and the swamp adder in particular.

Note: students will find that there is no such snake as a 'swamp adder', that snakes are deaf and do not care for milk. No snake could climb a bellrope without being trained to do so.

Martin Guerre, Part 1

Unit 4: Lesson 7

70 minutes approx.

Objectives

Word: (not listed) appreciate the specific meaning in context of an increasing range of words.

Reading: Rd6 comment on the authorial perspectives offered in texts on individuals, community and society in texts from different cultures – *sixteenth century France.*

Writing: Wr16 present a balanced analysis of a situation, text, issue or set of ideas, taking into account a range of evidence and opinions.

Speaking and Listening: S&L9 discuss and evaluate conflicting evidence to arrive at a considered viewpoint.

Word/Sentence Activity:

Students will find the following legal terminology helpful in understanding the text:

Appeal – the losing party in all other cases may appeal to a court of appeal, which will consider the course of the trial.

Cross-examination – the purpose of cross-examination is to test the evidence given, and an experienced lawyer seeks to weaken the credibility of damaging evidence and of the witness.

Defendant – the person who is accused.

Evidence – the means by which disputed facts are proved to be true or untrue in a trial.

Fraud – any means used by one person to deceive another may be defined as fraud.

Jury – a group of people who are chosen to decide the truth of factual evidence in a trial. Traditionally, a trial jury consists of 12 people.

Testimony – oral or written statement under oath

Witness – a person who testifies or gives evidence in a judicial proceeding or someone who is present at the execution of a legal document such as a will.

Introduction:

Shared reading of resource 35, The Martin Guerre Trials, Part 1.

Development:

Working in small groups of 2–3, students work through the 'Preparation and discussion' section of the resource sheet.

Plenary:

Go over the 'Preparation and discussion' tasks:

The purpose of the summary is to ensure that students have a good grasp of the basic facts.

Martin brought a lawsuit against Pierre, and though it was settled, Pierre remained angry.

Bertrande could have had many reasons: the return of a husband restored her rights of inheritance; she may have preferred any man to being lonely; she may have fallen in love with the imposter; she may have really thought that the man was Martin.

The appeal judge was less certain that the man was an imposter because of the testimony of witnesses, and the difference in personality between the man and Arnaud du Tilh.

Evidence that the man was Martin Guerre:

- He recognised family and neighbours.
- His sisters accepted him.
- Bertrande said he was her husband.
- Forty out of 150 witnesses said he was Martin Guerre.
- Bertrande would not denounce him.
- Jean Coras suspected a plot by Pierre.
- His character was very different from the character of Arnaud du Tilh.

Evidence that the man was an imposter:

- He was shorter and stockier than Martin Guerre.
- He spoke no Basque.
- A French solider said that the real Martin Guerre had lost a leg in battle.
- Several men said he was really Arnaud du Tilh.
- Fifty out of 150 witnesses said he was an imposter.

Homework:

Students choose one of the written tasks from the resource sheet.

Follow-up:

Research trial procedures. *Encarta* has an excellent helpful article on the modern British system.

35. The Martin Guerre Trials, Part 1

Martin Guerre Trials:

1560

Defendant: Martin Guerre (Arnaud du Tilh)
Crimes Charged: Defrauding the Guerre family and others and abusing Bertrande Guerre
Defense Lawyer: None
Prosecutors: King's attorneys
Judges: First trial: Firmin Vayssiere; second trial: Jean Coras (and others)
Places: First trial: Rieux, France; second trial: Toulouse, France
Dates of Trials: First trial: January–April 1560; second trial: May–September 12 1560
Verdicts: Both trials: Guilty
Sentences: First trial: Beheading and quartering; second trial: hanging and burning

SIGNIFICANCE: On one level, this is simply an exciting and curious case that allows everyone to speculate about human conduct and motives, especially those of the wife of Martin Guerre. For historians, however, it presents a unique opportunity to examine how common people of centuries past behaved and thought.

Sanxi Daguerre was a Basque. Basques live on the French-Spanish border. In 1527, Daguerre moved his wife, his young son, Martin, and his brother, Pierre, from the Atlantic coast 170 miles to the east. They settled in the French village of Artigat. The two brothers bought land and began a tile-manufacturing business. In order to blend in with their new neighbors they changed their name to Guerre and adopted the French language. A sign of the Guerre family's acceptance came in 1538 when Martin married Bertrande de Rols, the daughter of one of the region's wealthier families.

Martin was only thirteen years old. Bertrande was even younger. Their parents has 'arranged' the marriage. This was a common practice so that their families could more easily transfer property from the bride to the groom. During the first eight years of the marriage there were no children. Then in 1547, Bertrande gave birth to a son. By that time Bertrande had matured into a beautiful young woman. Martin, however, was a rather irresponsible young man. His strongest interest was swordplay and acrobatics with other village youths. He either rejected his family responsibilities, or simply wanted to see more of the world. In any event, in 1548, after he was accused of stealing some grain from his father, Martin disappeared.

The villagers considered Bertrande to be married to Martin until she could prove his death. As she could not, she remained financially dependent on his family. After Martin's parents died, Martin's uncle Pierre became the administrator of an estate that would have passed to Martin and his heirs, had Martin not vanished. Then, in 1556, eight years after he disappeared, Martin Guerre returned.

The New Martin Guerre

Perhaps it is more accurate to say that a man claiming to be Martin Guerre came to Artigat in 1556. He said that he had spent his time living in Spain and serving in the French army. However, he appeared to be shorter and stockier than the man who had vanished eight years earlier. What is more, he spoke no Basque. Time, he said, explained these oddities. However, he did seem to recognise his family and his neighbours. He knew many details about their pasts. Furthermore, his sisters accepted him. Most importantly, Bertrande said he was her husband.

Soon, their lives appeared to be perfectly normal. Bertrande gave birth to two more children. Martin increased their wealth by dealing in real estate. In 1559, however, things changed. Martin brought a lawsuit against his uncle, claiming that Pierre, as administrator of the family business, had cheated him and Bertrande. The suit was settled, but Pierre remained so angry that he went around town denouncing Martin as an imposter.

Some villagers agreed with Pierre. Just as many did not. Bertrande said: 'He is Martin Guerre my husband or else some devil in his skin. I know him well. Whoever is so mad as to say the contrary, I'll have him killed.' For a while, the villagers were satisfied.

Sometime in the fall [autumn] of 1559, though, a French soldier passing through Artigat said that Martin Guerre was an imposter. The soldier said that he knew the real Martin Guerre had lost a leg in battle two years earlier. Excited by this news, Pierre set about investigating the man who was living with Bertrande.

Very quickly Pierre located several men in the area who confirmed his suspicions. The imposter was really Arnaud du Tilh from the village of Sajas, 150 miles northwest of Artigat. Arnaud had as a youth been 'absorbed in every vice,' swearing, gambling, drinking, and frequenting prostitutes. His main gifts were his ability to persuade others with smooth talk and an excellent memory. These, of course, are the skills of an actor. After some trouble with the law, the young Arnaud had joined the king's army.

Although Arnaud would later deny it ever happened, it is possible that he met Martin Guerre during their military service in the mid-1550s and saw some resemblance between them. Arnaud claimed, however, that he had never met Martin Guerre. Instead, he declared that he had arrived at the idea of posing as Guerre after some of the other man's friends mixed the two men up. After he had learned as much as he could about Guerre, Arnaud went to Artigat and began a new life.

The First Trial

Armed with this information, Pierre Guerre personally arrested Arnaud in January 1560. Pierre then took him to the nearby village of Rieux, where the district court was located. What followed was more a judicial hearing than a modern trial. There was no jury, and Arnaud had no defense lawyer. First, the judge called an attorney for the king and court, and statements were taken from witnesses for both sides of the dispute. (Bertrande agreed to Pierre's demand that she join him in charging Arnaud as an imposter. She may also have supplied the names of witnesses who supported Arnaud.) Then the hearing began with the judge questioning Arnaud, Bertrande, and those witnesses who supported Pierre's charges.

Arnaud's cross-examination of the witnesses interested the judge. More people were called to testify. Eventually, some 150 witnesses appeared at the trial. About forty of these insisted that the prisoner was Martin Guerre. About fifty said he was an imposter. The remainder said they could not be sure. The most ambivalent testimony came from Bertrande, who was in effect on trial herself. If this man was an imposter, why had she gone along with him all these years? The defendant finally faced her and said he would accept a death sentence if she would swear under oath that he was not the real Martin Guerre. Bertrande remained silent.

In the end, the judge declared the defendant guilty of fraud and of abusing Bertrande.

Bertrande, as one of the plaintiffs in the suit, asked only that Arnaud pay a fine and legal fees and ask her pardon in a public ceremony. The judge, however, sentenced the prisoner to be beheaded and his body to be quartered (cut up and displayed). Arnaud du Tilh immediately appealed the decision.

The Second Trial

The new trial was before an appeals court of twelve judges. One of them, Jean Coras, acted as the lead judge. (It is his account of the case that serves as the primary source of information about the case.) Martin cross-examined Bertrande and Pierre. He was so convincing that the judges decided 'the prisoner was the true husband and that the imposture came from the side of the wife and the uncle.' Bertrande and Pierre, too, were placed in prison.

Twenty-five to thirty witnesses appeared during the following weeks. Jean Coras paid close attention to what they had to say. Gradually, he became less certain about the case against the alleged imposter. He became convinced that Pierre had forced Bertrande to turn against her husband. He also decided the Pierre was the true villain, motivated by a desire to get even with his nephew's request for a clear accounting of the family's finances. Coras disregarded claims that the defendant was Arnaud du Tilh. The testimony that Arnaud was 'given over to every kind of wickedness' proved that the upstanding individual before the court could not be that man. Finally, because the marriage had produced children, Coras decided that 'it was better to leave unpunished a guilty person than to condemn an innocent one.'

By late July, the court seemed ready to follow Coras's recommendation that Martin be found innocent and Pierre charged with various crimes.

From: *Courtroom Drama* by Frost-Knappman, Knappman & Paddock (eds)

PREPARATION AND DISCUSSION:

Write a summary of the events from Martin's disappearance up to the beginning of the trial.

What could have been Pierre's motives for claiming that the man was not Martin Guerre?

What could have been Bertrande's motives for her actions, i.e. for accepting the man as her husband, and later, for agreeing to press charges against him?

Why do you think she refused to swear under oath that the man was not Martin Guerre?

Why was the appeal judge 'less certain' about the case against the man?

Highlight all the evidence which supports the man's claim to be Martin Guerre.

In another colour, highlight all the evidence that suggests the man is an imposter.

WRITING:

Imagine that you are a lawyer for the defence OR the prosecution at the Second Trial. Plan the case that you would present to Judge Jean Coras, i.e.

- Which witnesses would you call?

- How would you question them?

- What would you say in your summing up speech?

Martin Guerre Part 2

Unit 4: Lesson 8

70 minutes approx.

Objectives

Sentence: (not listed) reflect on how their knowledge of other languages enhances their understanding of English.

Reading: Rd6 comment on the authorial perspectives offered in texts on individuals, community and society in texts from different cultures.

Writing: Wr16 present a balanced analysis of a situation, text, issue or set of ideas, taking into account a range of evidence and opinions.

Word/Sentence Activity:

Students investigate links between French and English by making a table of related words in the text 'Arrest du Parlement' on resource 36, e.g:

FRENCH	ENGLISH
arrest	arrest
contenant	containing
histoire	history/story
memorable	memorable
etc.	etc.

If time allows, students could calculate the percentage of words which have similarities.

Introduction:

Shared reading of resource 37, The Martin Guerre Trials, Part 2.

Development:

Working in small groups of 2–3, students work through the 'Preparation and discussion' section of the resource sheet.

Plenary:

Go over the 'Preparation and discussion' tasks:

The Guerre family accepted him without question.
Bertrande asked him for forgiveness.

He seems less clear on details about Artigat. However, the evidence that he is the real Martin Guerre is overwhelming.

Bertrande's actions were the most important in influencing the judge's decision.

The sentence on Arnaud is harsh by modern standards. Bertrande is treated leniently, and Coras's doubts about Pierre's motives seem to have been forgotten.

The best defence would probably be to appeal against the harshness of the sentence and to accuse Pierre of conspiracy to defraud Bertrande.

Homework:

Students do the written tasks from the resource sheet: write the secret diary of Bertande Guerre. Explain that they can use their imaginations freely as long as the diary fits the basic facts of the trial.

Follow-up:

Re-run the trial. In order to involve more students it would be a good idea to adopt lawyers for the defence and prosecution. In this way, it would be possible to involve half the class, with the other half as the audience. If time allows, roles could switched so that the audience had a turn to re-run the trial.

PARTS:
A panel of judges
A lawyer for the defence
A lawyer for the prosecution
Arnaud
Bertande
Pierre
Martin
Usher
Witnesses

36. Arrest dv Parlement

ARREST DV PARLEMENT
de Tolofe, contenant vne hiftoire memorable,
& prodigieufe, auec cent belles & doɛtes
Annotations, de monfieur maiftre
JEAN DE CORAS, rap-
porteur du proces.
Texte de la toile du proces
& de l'arreft.

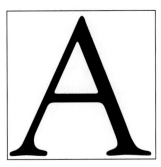

V moys de Januier, mil cinq cens cinquante neuf, Bertrande de Rolz, du lieu, d'Artigat, au diocefe de Rieux, fe rend fuppliant, & plaintiue, deuant le Iuge de Rieux: difant, que vingt ans peuuét eftre paffez, ou enuiron, qu'elle eftant ieune fille, de neuf à dix ans, fut mariee, auec Martin Guerre, pour lors aufsi fortieune, & prefque de mefmes aage, que la fuppliant.

Annotation I.

Les mariages ainfi contractez auant l'aage legitime, ordonné de nature, ou par les loix politiques, ne peuuent eftre (s'il eft loyfible de fonder, iufques aux fecretz, & inlcrutables jugemens de la diuinité) plaifans, ny aggreables à Dieu, & illue, en eit le plus fouuent piteufe, & miferable, & (comme on voit journellement par exemple) pleine, de mille repentances: partant qu'entelles precoces, & deuancces conionctions, ceux qui ont tramé, & proietté le tout, n'ont aucunement refpecté l'honneur, & la gloire de Dieu: & moins la fin, pour laquelle cefaint, & venerable eitat de mariage, ha cité par luy inititué du commencement du monde. A (qui fut deuant l'offence de noitre premier pere,
pour

From: *Courtroom Drama* by Frost-Knappman, Knappman & Paddock (eds)

37. The Martin Guerre Trials, Part 2

The Real Martin Guerre

Suddenly, out of nowhere came a man with a wooden leg claiming to be the real Martin Guerre. He said he had gone to Spain after leaving Artigat, where he worked as a servant before joining the Spanish army. He fought with them in Flanders (a region primarily located in Belgium) and lost his leg in the famous battle of Saint-Quentin in 1557. He then returned to Spain, where the military rewarded him with a job. It was not clear why he had returned to France.

The judges began a new round of hearings. At first, the new Martin Guerre seemed less clear on details about Artigat than did the alleged imposter. In the end, the judges were convinced when the Guerre family instantly accepted the newcomer as one of their own. The decisive moment came when Bertrande was brought from her cell. She fell to her knees before the new Martin Guerre, embraced him, and asked his forgiveness.

For Coras and the other judges, the case was over. All that was left was to decide on sentencing. The judges forgave Bertrande. They declared her children by Arnaud legitimate, that is, legally conceived. They also excused Pierre because he had been right in the end. They rebuked Martin for having deserted his family and country. Finally, though, they excused him as well. He had suffered enough. However, the judges sentenced Arnaud du Tilh to be hanged on a gallows to be built in front of Martin and Bertrande Guerre's home. Arnaud's final words urged Martin to be kind to Bertrande, who had truly been deceived.

Nothing more is known of Martin and Bertrande, except that they had two more children. In all the centuries that have passed since the return of Martin Guerre, no one has been able to discover the truth of Bertrande's role in the case.

From: *Courtroom Drama* by Frost-Knappman, Knappman & Paddock (eds)

PREPARATION AND DISCUSSION:

Highlight evidence which suggests that the man with the wooden leg is the real Martin Guerre.

Highlight any evidence which suggests that he is not.

What was it that most infuenced the judges' final decision?

Do you agree with the judges' sentences on Arnaud du Tihl, Bertrande and Pierre?

Imagine that the other man decides to take his case to an appeal court and you have been asked to speak in his defence – what would you say?

WRITING:

Write 'The Secret Diary of Bertrande Guerre' in which you reveal what really happened.

Martin Guerre – the Musical

Unit 4: Lesson 9

70 minutes approx.

Objectives

Word: (not listed) appreciate the specific meaning in context of an increasing range of words.

Reading: Rd8 analyse how media texts influence and are influenced by readers.

Writing: Wr16 present a balanced analysis of a situation, text, issue or set of ideas, taking into account a range of evidence and opinions.

Notes:

For best effect, this lesson needs a recording of the latest version of *Martin Guerre*. The Boublil and Schönberg Musical, 4th Version (UK/US Tours) – November 1998–Present.

The musical can be studied in two ways a) a short sample (using the excerpt on resource 38, All that I love), or b) in full (the libretto can be downloaded from: http://www.crosswinds.net/~charivari/mgleedsact2.html and can be printed on ten sides of A4 (using two columns)).

Word/Sentence Activity:

Introduce students to the term *ambiguous* – a statement which has a double meaning or is vague.

Explain to students that there are many types of ambiguity (William Empson, in a famous critical work, identified seven). The two main types are:

a) statements which are ambiguous because they are badly written

b) statements which are deliberately ambiguous for a particular reason – this type of ambiguity is frequently used by authors.

Introduction:

Listen to as much of the musical as possible. As a minimum, listen to 'All that I Love' and 'The Final Witness'.

Development:

In small groups of 4–6, students read the lyrics to these songs. They should then discuss the questions that follow.

Plenary:

Go over the discussion questions.

The storyline is simplified, and in some cases changed, for example, it is Arnaud who finally admits the truth, not Bertrande.

The words by themselves seem quite simple, but the music adds drama, tension and emotion.

Note: if students are studying the full version they will see that the ending is very different. Also, throughout the musical, the conflict between the Protestants and the Catholics has a large part to play.

Homework:

(Only after study of the whole musical) Write a review of *Martin Guerre*. Why do you think this musical has been less successful that *Les Miserables* and *Miss Saigon* by the same authors?

Follow-up:

Try to see one of the film versions of this story:

Le Retour de Martin Guerre
A 1982 French film starring Gerard Depardieu as Arnaud du Tihl and Nathalie Baye as Bertrande de Rols.
Sommersby
A 1993 American remake of *Le Retour de Martin Guerre*, set just after the Civil War and starring Richard Gere and Jodie Foster.

38. All That I Love

BERTRANDE
It is easy to say
Just as night becomes day
The truth's here before me for

All that I love, all that I know
In God's name I swear
This is the man I gave my life to

All that I love, all that I trust
Is here to stay beside me
And the child that will bear his
Name

I prayed for the day he would grow
To be strong
The day he would know he could
Love and belong
He answered my prayers, who can say
Love is wrong?

All that I need, all that I've planned
Returned to his land and made my
Life worth living
All that I love

ARNAUD
I will always be here

BERTRANDE
All that I know

ARNAUD
Let a new life begin

BERTRANDE
All that I need

BERTRANDE AND ARNAUD
That I knew
From the start
Would belong
In my heart
All that is true
All that is strong
I'll spend my life loving you

JUDGE
Words
Words of love
Where's the truth?
Your love is true, this I see
This is not what justice needs to know
For still all we need is his name
There is no one to speak
There is nothing to say
The night is full of questions
The answers will come with the day

The USHER evacuates the courtroom. The JUDGE sits alone at his desk.

The Final Witness

JUDGE
Never have I heard such a pitiful case
The law demands dignity, never disgrace
I have heard all you've said, ev'ry lie ev'ry grudge
On the word of one man there is no case to judge.

USHER
Please, your honour, if I may . . .
There's a man, won't go away
Travelled far and wants a word
Claims his story should be heard

JUDGE
What's his name?

USHER
He won't say

JUDGE
Let him in . . .
Your name. State your name.

MARTIN
My name is Guerre. Martin Guerre.

MARTIN is interrogated but still the Judge is not satisfied.

JUDGE
Bertrande, you've listened to these men
We need the truth, the time has come.

PIERRE
I knew the truth, I knew my blood.

GUILLAUME
The truth is all she needs is me.

BERTRANDE (to Arnaud)
If you have lied to me ...
Have you lied to me?
No, you would not lie

MADAME DE ROLS
He's lied to us all, Bertrande
Now tell us the truth.

THE WHOLE VILLAGE
We need the truth, we need it now.

BERTRANDE
The truth is not enough
The truth does not explain
The truth ... what is the truth?

MADAME DE ROLS
My little girl ...

JUDGE
Tell us, Bertrande

THE WHOLE VILLAGE
Tell us the truth ...

ARNAUD
I am Arnaud du Tilh.

DISCUSSION:

* Bertrande's statement in 'All That I Love' is a good example of ambiguity because it has a double meaning – what are the two different meanings in her statement?

* Why is she deliberately ambiguous?

* What does Bertrande mean when she says in 'The Final Witness', 'The truth is not enough?

* What changes did Schonberg and Boulbil make to the original story?

* How does the music add to the emotional impact?

* As far as you can judge from these two songs, and your knowledge of the overall story, why do you think *Martin Guerre* has not been as successful as *Les Miserables* and *Miss Saigon* which are by the same authors?

Detective Story Cards

Unit 4: Lesson 10

70 minutes approx.

Objectives

Word: various.

Sentence: various.

Writing: (not listed) reveal character, establish settings and develop narrative through an effective mix of action, dialogue, description and commentary.

Speaking and Listening: S&L9 discuss and evaluate conflicting evidence to arrive at a considered viewpoint.

Word/Sentence Activity:

In a question and answer session, revise the following key story writing skills.

- use of adjectives and adverbs to develop description
- basic speech punctuation and how to develop dialogue
- paragraph openings and organisation
- story planning
- writing effective beginnings and endings.

See Unit 1, 'Global Tales' for specific resources to develop the above skills.

Introduction:

Recap on the features of a typical detective story by displaying resource 32, *The Hound of the Baskervilles* as a detective story on OHP.

Development:

Explain to students that they are going to write their own detective stories using the detective story cards to help them. There are two ways to use the detective story cards:

1) Students work in pairs and use the cards as a planning aid. They should work through resource 39, Detective Story Cards – Planner, discussing various alternatives, until both of them have a plan for a detective story.

2) Students work in groups of 7–8 and use the cards in a story-telling game. The first step is to enlarge the cards to A3 size and then cut them out (they could also be mounted and laminated to create a reusable resource). Note that the Characters and Settings cards from the Story Kit (Unit 1) can be used to give more choice of characters and some ideas for settings. When the cards are prepared, students follow these instructions:

- Shuffle each set of cards, CHARACTERS, CRIMES, MOTIVES, OBJECTS, CLUES, ALIBIS and RED HERRINGS, and place the sets face down in the middle of the table (alternatively, each group member can hold one of the sets).

- The first player takes the top card from each set and places them face up in front of him.

- Another two characters should be chosen (or dealt) from the CHARACTERS set.

- The player must make up an oral story using all the cards.

Tips for preparing the story:

- The story should be told in the *first person*.
- Look at the three PEOPLE cards and choose a *victim* – this can be anybody.
- The victim will be a victim of the crime on the CRIME card.
- Choose two *suspects*. One should be the *criminal*, the other should be a *red herring*. The red herring should seem to be the obvious suspect – he/she should look evil, should have a poor alibi, and should behave suspiciously. The real criminal should be less obvious.
- The other cards (MOTIVE, OBJECT, CLUE, ALIBI, RED HERRING) should be used for ideas to build up the rest of the story.
- Where possible, all the cards should be referred to in the story. However, if one card is a bad fit to the others, it may be left out.
- Continue the game clockwise around the table.
- When everyone has had a turn, decide whose was the best story.
- The rest of the group should then help that person to prepare the story for presentation to the class or other groups.

Plenary:

Selected students present their plans to the rest of the class OR a representative from each group tells an oral detective story to the rest of the class.

Homework:

Students produce a written version of their detective story.

Follow-up:

Use the redrafting cards from Unit 1 (resource 10) to develop and redraft the story.

39. Detective Story Cards – Planner

1. From the character cards, choose a character to be the detective. Develop the character of the detective by giving him or her interests, eccentricities and a particular method of solving crimes.

2. From the character cards, choose a villain. TIP: Don't choose an 'obvious' villain – go for one that is smart or sophisticated-looking.

3. From the character cards, choose a red-herring character. TIP: This person should look villainous. The reader of the story should suspect this character instead of the real villain.

4. From the crime cards, select a crime. Develop this by selecting a victim from the character cards, and by creating an appropriate setting.

5. From the motive cards, select a motive. This is important as it could lead to the detection of the criminal.

6. From the object cards, select some objects which will be used to commit the crime.

7. From the alibi cards, select a plausible alibi for the villain, and a poor alibi for the red-herring character.

8. Add to the complexity of the story by choosing another red herring to distract the reader's attention from the real villain.

9. Work out a solution to the crime. Note that the solution must follow from the motives, clues, alibis, etc. A good detective story contains enough clues for the reader to guess the solution, but not enough to make guessing the solution easy.

10. Redraft and proofread the story.

40. Detective Story Cards 1 & 2

MALE CHARACTERS

BEN	DICK	HARRY
JAMES	PAUL	TOM

FEMALE CHARACTERS

CHLOE	JENNY	JUDY
MANDY	SHARON	TRUDY

Detective Story Cards 3 & 4

CRIMES

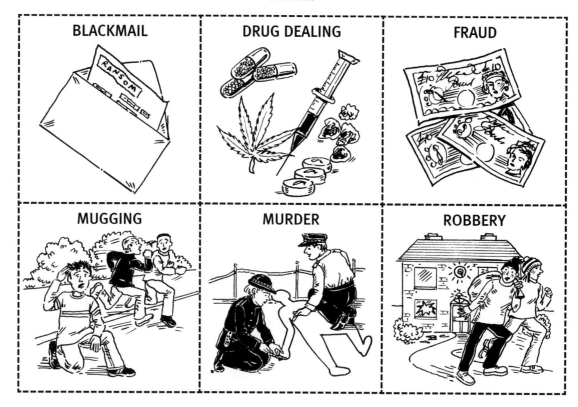

BLACKMAIL	DRUG DEALING	FRAUD
MUGGING	MURDER	ROBBERY

MOTIVES

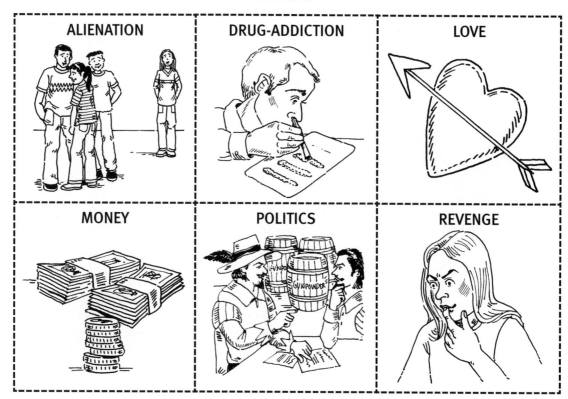

ALIENATION	DRUG-ADDICTION	LOVE
MONEY	POLITICS	REVENGE

Detective Story Cards 5 & 6

OBJECTS

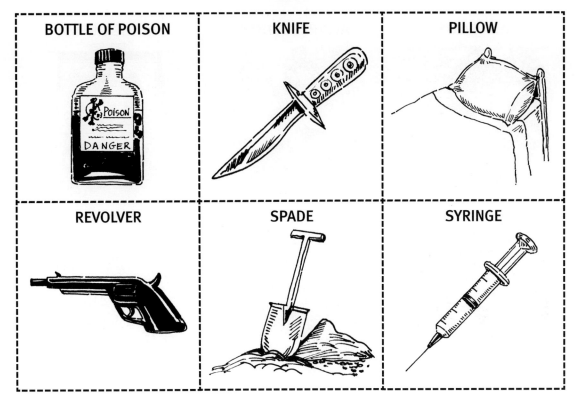

CLUES

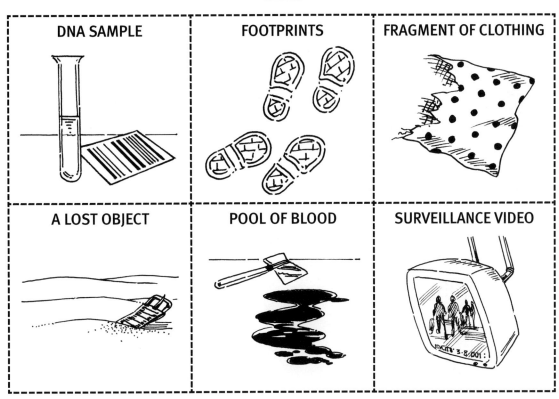

Detective Story Cards 7 & 8

ALIBIS

AT A PARTY	AT A RESTAURANT	AT THE CINEMA

AT THE DENTIST'S	AT WORK	VISITING AGED GRANDPARENT
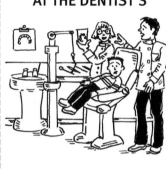		

RED HERRINGS

A CHARACTER WITH A STRONG MOTIVE	A MISLEADING CLUE	A PREVIOUS CRIME WHICH IS SIMILAR

A VILLAINOUS CHARACTER	AN APPARENTLY FOOLPROOF ALIBI	THE POLICE MAKE AN ARREST

UNIT 5: MODERN POETRY

Title of unit: MODERN POETRY

Resources
Books: Any anthology of modern poetry to supplement the poems reproduced in this unit; *The Dread Affair*, Benjamin Zephaniah, Arena, ISBN 009939250X.

Year: 9	Term: 3, first half	Duration: 8 lessons	Set: All

NLS objectives		NC objectives
War: 'I Vow To Thee My Country' and 'Disabled'	Rd12, Wr17, S&L10	En1 6e) the vocabulary and grammar of standard English and dialect variation.
City Life: 'Rhapsody on a Windy Night' and 'Bukit Timah, Singapore'	Wd7, Rd18, Wr17, S&L9	En2 8c) poetry by major writers from different cultures and traditions.
Work: 'Toads' and 'Follower'	Wd8, Rd17, Wr17	En2 8a) vi) poetry by four major poets published after 1914.
Experiments	Wd7, Rd16, Wr17, S&L9	En3 1 writing to analyse, review, comment.
Benjamin Zephaniah	Sn10, Rd16, S&L9	En3 1 writing to imagine, explore, entertain.
Issues	Sn10, Rd16, Wr13	
Black English	Rd16, Wr9	
Writing About a Poet	Wd6, Rd16, Wr17	

Teaching sequence	Outcomes
Week 1: War: 'I Vow To Thee My Country' and 'Disabled' City Life: 'Rhapsody on a Windy Night' and 'Bukit Timah, Singapore'	*Write an essay using the template. *Write about a poem with a particular focus on poetic techniques.
Week 2: Work: 'Toads' and 'Follower' Experiments	*Write about a poem with a particular focus on themes. Write own experimental poem.
Week 3: Benjamin Zephaniah Issues	Write an account of Standard English and compare it with Zephaniah's English. Write a newspaper article based on the ideas in 'Modern Slavery'.
Week 4: Black English Writing about a poet	Further research into black English. *Write an essay on Zephaniah's poetry.
	*Assessment pieces

Note: most lessons include the study of two poems – which is about right for a lesson of 70 minutes. However, if desired, it is possible to teach the main skills using one of the poems in a single lesson of 35 minutes.

War

Unit 5: Lesson 1

70 minutes approx.

Objectives

Reading: Rd12 analyse and discuss the use made of rhetorical devices in a text.

Writing: Wr17 cite specific and relevant textual evidence to justify critical judgements about texts.

Speaking and Listening: S&L10 contribute to the organisation of group activity in ways that help to structure plans, solve problems and evaluate alternatives.

Starter Activity:

Using resource 41, Use of Evidence, revise the importance of supporting key points with evidence.

Introduction:

Because of its strong themes and powerful language, war poetry is a good introduction to modern poetry. The two poems in this selection have been chosen to provide a contrast between 'jingoistic' attitudes to war and the realities of war.

Shared reading of 'I Vow to Thee My Country' and 'Disabled' (resources 43 and 44).

Development:

Students, working in small groups of 2–3, discuss the questions after each poem.

The next step is to write notes on 'Disabled' on resource 42, Template for Writing About a Poem. Explain to students that this template has been designed for general use, and that further work will be done on each section. For the moment, they should comment on any poetic techniques they know in section 2, particularly metaphor and simile. The resource 'Poetic techniques' will be introduced next lesson, and will help them to go into greater detail when they use this resource in the future. Ask students to include a paragraph comparing this poem with 'I Vow to Thee My Country' – a suitable place would be when discussing themes in section 3.

Plenary:

Go over the discussion questions and the notes made on resource 42, Template for writing about a poem.

Homework:

Use the notes on resource 42, Template for Writing About a Poem, as the basis for writing an essay.

Follow-up:

Encourage students to read more of Wilfred Owen's poems. More poems and useful biographical information can be found at:

http://bewoner.dma.be/ericlaer/cultural/owen.html

To help students understand the horrors of World War I, show all or part of *All Quiet on the Western Front* (1930) based upon the 1929 novel by Erich Maria Remarque, and directed by Lewis Milestone.

41. Use of Evidence

When writing about literary texts it is important to support the key points with evidence from the text. Read this short example and the notes below.

> The second verse goes beyond pride in country because it is about 'another country'. This refers to a spiritual dimension, probably heaven. The poet says that the values in that country are the opposite of the militaristic values implied by fighting for one's country, e.g. faithfulness. It is a place which is the opposite of war-torn Europe:
>
> 'And her ways are ways of gentleness and all her paths are peace.'

NOTES:

- The first point is supported by a short quotation. Quotations which are less than a line in length should be run into the text. Short quotations of this kind are the most useful. They are easy to remember, and provide evidence in an efficient and effective way.

- The third sentence contains an example of indirect evidence. The student refers to a specific part of the text but without quoting the actual words.

- The last example is a complete line of poetry. Quotations which are one whole line or more should be set out with a blank line before and after them and indented. It is not necessary to use many quotations which are more than two lines long – indeed it is regarded by most teachers and examiners as mere 'padding'. The important skill is to identify the phrase or line which supports the point.

TASK:

Look over a recent literary essay with a partner, and find places where you could have made better use of evidence.

42. Template for Writing About a Poem

NOTES ON: **BY:**

SUBJECT – briefly explain what the poem is about (evidence is not necessary in this section).

POETIC TECHNIQUES – comment on the main poetic techniques (see resource 45). Give evidence from the text.

THEME – discuss the ideas which the poet is exploring. Give evidence from the text.

OTHER
Write about anything else not included above, e.g. the focus of a specific question, a comparison with another poem, important background information, etc. Give evidence where appropriate.

43. I Vow To Thee My Country

I Vow To Thee My Country

I vow to thee, my country, all earthly things above,
Entire and whole and perfect, the service of my love:
The love that asks no question, the love that stands the test,
That lays upon the altar the dearest and the best;
The love that never falters, the love that pays the price,
The love that makes undaunted the final sacrifice.

And there's another country, I've heard of long ago,
Most dear to them that love her, most great to them that know;
We may not count her armies, we may not see her King;
Her fortress is a faithful heart, her pride is suffering;
And soul by soul and silently her shining bounds increase,
And her ways are ways of gentleness and all her paths are peace.

Cecil Spring-Rice (1859–1918)
Sung to tune 'Thaxted' by Gustav Holst (1874–1934)

Note: the tune can be heard online at:
http://tch.simplenet.com/htm/i/v/ivow2the.htm

Cecil Spring-Rice

DISCUSSION:

⬤ Analyse the verse form by counting stressed syllables in each line and noting the rhyme scheme.

⬤ What attitudes to country are expressed in this poem?

⬤ What can you deduce about Cecil Spring-Rice and the values he holds from his photograph?

⬤ Do you think that patriotism is a good thing?

⬤ What 'other country' is referred to in the second verse?

44. *Disabled*

Disabled

He sat in a wheeled chair, waiting for dark,
And shivered in his ghastly suit of grey,
Legless, sewn short at elbow. Through the park
Voices of boys rang saddening like a hymn,
Voices of play and pleasure after day,
Till gathering sleep had mothered them from him.

About this time Town used to swing so gay
When glow-lamps budded in the light blue trees,
And girls glanced lovelier as the air grew dim –
In the old times, before he threw away his knees.
Now he will never feel again how slim
Girls' waists are, or how warm their subtle hands;
All of them touch him like some queer disease.

There was an artist silly for his face,
For it was younger than his youth, last year.
Now, he is old; his back will never brace;
He's lost his colour very far from here,
Poured it down shell-holes till the veins ran dry,
And half his lifetime lapsed in the hot race
And leap of purple spurted from his thigh.

One time he liked a blood-smear down his leg,
After the matches, carried shoulder-high.
It was after football, when he'd drunk a peg,
He thought he'd better join – He wonders why.
Someone had said he'd look a god in kilts,
That's why; and may be, too, to please his Meg;
Aye, that was it, to please the giddy jilts
He asked to join. He didn't have to beg;
Smiling they wrote his lie; aged nineteen years.
Germans he scarcely thought of; all their guilt,
And Austria's, did not move him. And no fears
Of Fear came yet. He thought of jewelled hilts
For daggers in plaid socks; of smart salutes;
And care of arms; and leave; and pay arrears;
Esprit de corps; and hints for young recruits.
And soon, he was drafted out with drums and cheers.

Some cheered him home, but not as crowds cheer Goal.
Only a solemn man who brought him fruits
Thanked him; and then inquired about his soul.

Now, he will spend a few sick years in institutes,
And do what things the rules consider wise,
And take whatever pity they may dole.
To-night he noticed how the women's eyes
Passed from him to the strong men that were whole.
How cold and late it is! Why don't they come
And put him into bed? Why don't they come?

Wilfred Owen (1893–1918)

DISCUSSION:

- Re-read stanza 4 and explain the young man's reason's for joining up. Do you think these were sensible reasons?

- Describe the young man's present condition.

- What life experiences has the young man lost out on because of his wounds?

- What message is Owen trying to get across by describing this young man's suffering so graphically?

- Explore the use of figurative language in the poem.

- Compare the attitudes to fighting for one's country with those expressed in 'I Vow to Thee My Country'.

WRITING:

Make notes about this poem on resource 56, Template for writing about a poem.

City life

Unit 5: Lesson 2

70 minutes approx.

Objectives

Word: Wd7 recognise layers of meaning in the writer's choice of words, e.g. *allusion*.

Reading: Rd18 discuss a substantial prose text, sharing perceptions, negotiating common readings and accounting for differences of view.

Writing: Wr17 cite specific and relevant textual evidence to justify critical judgements about texts.

Speaking and Listening: S&L9 discuss and evaluate conflicting evidence to arrive at a considered viewpoint.

Word/Sentence Activity:

Using resource 45, Poetic Techniques, revise key terms for poetic techniques and teach new terms as necessary. One way to do this is to fold resource 45 so that only the terms are photocopied and to ask students to write a short definition for each term. This will reveal what students know, what they have a vague idea about, and what they don't know at all.

Explain to students that there are, of course, many more terms describing poetic techniques, but that this is a useful 'toolkit' of terms for Year 9. Less able students should be asked to try to learn the most essential which are *simile, metaphor* and *imagery*.

Finally, draw students' attention to the important note at the bottom of the sheet.

Introduction:

Shared reading of 'Rhapsody on a Windy Night' and 'Bukit Timah'.

Development:

Students, in groups of 3–4, discuss the questions following each poem. Note that the questions should be simplified for the less able (e.g. by leaving out some of the more difficult poetic terms).

The next step is for students to make notes on the poems using resource 42, Template for Writing About a Poem.

Plenary:

Go over the discussion questions:

Notes:
'Rhapsody on a Windy Night' is an excellent example of the powerful effect of these poetic techniques in the hands of a great poet.

Ambiguity – the whole poem is ambiguous. It describes the mental state of a person, but the person's specific problem is never made clear.

Free verse – the poem is written in free verse. The mixture of long and short lines and the lack of predictable pattern is an appropriate reflection of the subject's mental state. Also, use of free verse is appropriate as it is a modern verse form used to describe a modern situation (alienation in city life).

Irony – the last two lines are ironic (as well as a paradox) because sleep, the preparation for the next day's life, is seen as the worst thing of all.

Metaphor – many examples, e.g. 'memory throws up high and dry'

Personification – the lamps whisper and speak, the moon winks and smiles etc.

Simile – many examples, e.g. 'the corner of her eye/Twists like a crooked pin.'

Symbol – the third stanza contains a series of symbols – these are strange, broken objects which stand for the strange things in the person's mind.

Students can be helped to write about the above techniques by giving them a pattern to follow. The following example describes a simile. It is in three parts: 1) an introductory sentence; 2) a quotation from the text; and 3) an explanation.

The poet uses a simile to describe the effect of midnight on the person's memory:

> *Midnight shakes the memory*
> *As a madman shakes a dead geranium.*

He says that midnight is affecting the memory of the person in the poem physically. The effect of this is to help us understand that the person in the poem is suffering from mental illness.

'Bukit Timah, Singapore' uses a range of poetic techniques, the most important of which is extended metaphor. This is explained below using the recommended pattern:

The poet uses an extended metaphor to describe the city. He uses words and phrases such as 'megalopolitan appetite' which has to be 'fed' with 'men, machines'. The poet also uses the terms 'gullet', 'feed' and 'disgorge' to describe the city. He is saying that the city is a monster that feeds on people. The effect of this is to make the city seem a fearful place which feeds on people rather than serves their needs.

Homework:

Ask students to choose one of the poems to write about in detail using the notes they made on resource 42, Template for Writing About a Poem. Encourage them to give particular emphasis to section 2, Poetic Techniques.

Follow-up:

There are many other terms for poetic techniques. Find out about the following:

Alexandrine	Parody
Assonance	Scansion
Metonomy	Synechdoche
Onomatopeia	Trochaic

Most of these terms will be needed relatively infrequently, so the main thing is to know where to find out about them. Definitions of the terms in the above list and many others can be found at:

http://www.clearcf.uvic.ca/writersguide/Pages/LiteraryTermsTOC.html

45. Poetic Techniques

Alliteration	Words beginning with the same sound, e.g. 'A fair field full of folk' (Langland)
Allusion	A reference to a well-known person or thing, e.g. 'My son Telemachus...' (Tennyson) is a reference to a character in Homer's *Odyssey*.
Ambiguity	Ambiguous or vague meaning is a fault in ordinary writing, but poets sometimes use it deliberately to make you think.
Diction	A poet's choice of words. When writing about diction, comment on adjectives, powerful verbs, archaic words, slang or dialect words and any other unusual or interesting words.
Figure of speech	Anything which is not literally true. The main ones are in this list, e.g. *simile, metaphor, personification*.
Free verse	A poetic form with no rhythm or rhyme.
Half-rhyme	The consonants are the same, the vowel sound is different, e.g. 'leaves/lives'.
Imagery	A blanket term which includes all figures of speech which are 'word pictures' particularly *simile* and *metaphor*.
Irony	Expressing something by saying the opposite, e.g. saying 'You're a big help!' to someone who breaks a dish while helping to wash up.
Metaphor	A direct comparison, e.g. 'A black hole'; 'My hands are ice', An **Extended metaphor** develops a metaphor with more ideas from the same comparison, e.g. '... and my fingers are icicles.'
Pentameter	Five stress line, e.g. 'Shall **I** com**pare** thee **to** a **sum**mer's **day**?'
Personification	Describing an object as though it had human qualities, for example, a famous sonnet by John Donne begins 'Death, be not proud ...'.
Rhyme	Word endings which sound the same, e.g. 'bed/instead'.
Simile	A comparison using *like* or *as*, e.g. 'My hands are as cold as ice'; 'Flight 19 disappeared as though it had gone to Mars.'
Sonnet	A set pattern of 14 rhyming pentameters. There are several different rhyme-schemes.
Symbol	Something that stands for something else, e.g. a skull can be used as a symbol for death, a heart for love, etc.

Important note: always remember that it is not enough merely to identify a poetic technique (which would reduce the study of poetry to the level of trainspotting). The important thing is to say what effect the technique has. The following pattern, which can be adapted to fit most of the above terms, will help you to do this:

INTRODUCTORY SENTENCE USING THE CORRECT TERM	A DETAILED EXPLANATION OF HOW THE POET USES IT	AN ANALYSIS OF WHAT EFFECT IT HAS
The poet uses *personification* to describe death. *Insert a quotation from the text.*	He says that death has the human quality of pride.	The effect of this is to make death seem less fearful. By giving it human qualities, Donne makes us feel we can fight back.

46. Rhapsody on a Windy Night

Rhapsody on a Windy Night

Twelve o'clock.
Along the reaches of the street
Held in a lunar synthesis.
Whispering lunar incantations
Dissolve the floors of memory
And all its clear relations.
Its divisions and precisions.
Every street lamp that I pass
Beats like a fatalistic drum.
And through the spaces of the dark
Midnight shakes the memory
As a madman shakes a dead geranium.

Half-past one.
The street-lamp sputtered.
The street-lamp muttered.
The street-lamp said, 'Regard that woman
Who hesitates toward you in the light of the door
Which opens on her like a grin.
You see the border of her dress
Is torn and stained with sand,
And you see the corner of her eye
Twists like a crooked pin.'

The memory throws up high and dry
A crowd of twisted things:
A twisted branch upon the beach
Eaten smooth, and polished
As if the world gave up
The secret of its skeleton.
Stiff and white.
A broken spring in a factory yard.
Rust that clings to the form that the strength has left
Hard and curled and ready to snap.

Half-past two.
The street-lamp said,
'Remark the cat which flattens itself in the gutter.
Slips out its tongue
And devours a morsel of rancid butter.'
So the hand of the child, automatic.
Slipped out and pocketed a toy that was running along the quay.
I could see nothing behind that child's eye.
I have seen eyes in the street
Trying to peer through lighted shutters.
And a crab one afternoon in a pool.

An old crab with barnacles on his back,
Gripped the end of a stick which I held him.

Half-past three,
The lamp sputtered,
The lamp muttered in the dark.
The lamp hummed:
'Regard the moon,
La lune ne garde aucune rancune.
She winks a feeble eye.
She smiles into corners.
She smooths the hair of the grass.
The moon has lost her memory.
A washed-out smallpox cracks her face,
Her hand twists a paper rose,
That smells of dust and eau de Cologne.
She is alone
With all the old nocturnal smells
That cross and cross across her brain.
The reminiscence comes
Of sunless dry geraniums
And dust in crevices,
Smells of chestnuts in the streets,
And female smells in shuttered rooms,
And cigarettes in corridors
And cocktail smells in bars.

The lamp said,
'Four o'clock.
Here is the number on the door.
Memory!
You have the key.
The little lamp spread a ring on the stair.
Mount.
The bed is open: the tooth-brush hangs on the wall.
Put your shoes at the door, sleep, prepare for life.'

The last twist of the knife.

T.S. Eliot

DISCUSSION:

- Find examples of the following poetic techniques: ambiguity, free verse, irony, metaphor, personification, simile, symbol.

- Explain the effect of any two different techniques using the pattern on resource 45.

- Describe in your own words the mental state of the person in the poem.

- How does Eliot's use of poetic techniques help to convey this mental state to the reader?

47. *Bukit Timah*, Singapore

Bukit Timah, Singapore

This highway I know,
the only way into the city
where the muddy canal goes.
These are the sides of coarse grasses
where the schoolboys stumble in early morning
wet-staining their white shoes.

This is the way the city is fed
men, machines,
flushed out of their short dreams
and suburban holes
to churn down this waiting gullet.
They flow endlessly this way
from dawn, before sky opens,
to the narrow glare of noon
and evening's slow closing.

Under the steaming morning,
ambition flashes by in a new car:
the reluctant salesman faced
with another day of selling his pride
hunches over the lambretta, swerving
from old farmer with fruit-heavy basket.
The women back from market
remark that this monsoon will be bad
for the price of vegetables:
their loitering children, too small for school,
learn the value of five cents, ten cents,
from hunger and these market days.

All morning the tired buses whine
their monotonous route, drag
from stop to stop,
disgorge schoolchildren, pale-faced clerks,
long-suffering civil servants,
pretty office girls, to feed
the megalopolitan appetite.

This highway I know,
the only way out of the city:
the same highway under the moon,
the same people under the sea-green
of lamps newly turned on at evening.

One day there will be tall buildings
here, where the green trees reach
for the narrow canal.
The holes where the restless sleepers are
will be neat, boxed up in ten-stories.
Life will be orderly, comfortable,
exciting, occasionally, at the new nightclubs.

I wonder what that old farmer would say
if he lived to come this way.

Lee Tzu Pheng

DISCUSSION:

- Find examples of the following poetic techniques: diction, free verse, irony, metaphor, extended metaphor, personification.

- Explain the effect of any two different techniques using the pattern on resource 42.

- What is Lee Tzu Pheng's main message about Singapore? How does his use of poetic techniques help to convey this?

Work

Unit 5: Lesson 3

70 minutes approx.

Objectives

Word: Wd8 recognise how lines of thought are developed and signposted through the use of connectives, e.g. *nonetheless, consequently, furthermore.*

Reading: Rd17 compare the themes and styles of two or more poets.

Writing: Wr17 cite specific and relevant textual evidence to justify critical judgements about texts.

Word/Sentence Activity:

Using resource 48, Qualifiers, revise some of the main techniques of qualifying nouns.

Introduction:

Shared reading of 'Toads' and 'Follower' (resources 50 and 51).

Development:

Students, in groups of 3–4, discuss the questions following each poem.

The next step is for students to make notes on the poems using resource 49, Themes. Point out that a personal response (see Section 3) will be an important feature when writing about poetry for GCSE.

Plenary:

Go over the discussion questions.

Notes:
The main ideas in 'Toads' are a) that work is unpleasant (reinforced by poetic techniques such as the metaphor 'sickening poison') and b) that Larkin does not have the courage not to do without it. Many students may find the latter idea hard to empathise with!

I have to admit that I've taught this poem for years and I don't understand the last verse! (answers on a postcard please). What 'both' is Larkin referring to?

The poem 'Followers' appears to be a description of his father's work as a ploughman. The technical terms such as 'steel-pointed sock' and 'headrig' show that Heaney had first-hand knowledge of ploughing. In the last two verses some new ideas are introduced and we see that the main theme of the poem is growing up. The last verse is a good example of *ambiguity* as it can mean several different things:

- The poet is now the mature man, his father the inferior 'follower' because of his decline into old age.

- It could refer to Heaney's achievement in his chosen field of poetry (in Ireland he is known as 'famous Seamus') in which he surpassed his father in his own chosen field.

- Taking the last two verses together, it is also about finding one's role. As a ploughman, Heaney could only be inferior – a 'follower' – whereas, in the field of poetry, it is his father who is inferior.

Discuss students' personal responses to the poems.

Homework:

Choose one of the poems to write about in detail using resource 42, Template for Writing About a Poem, as a basis. Encourage students to give particular attention to Section 3, 'Themes'.

Follow-up:

Read 'Toads Revisited' to find out how Philip Larkin changed his views on work in later life.

48. Qualifiers

Qualifiers are words, phrases or clauses which can be used to *qualify* (viz. add further information to) nouns or pronouns.

Prepositional phrases

For example: . . . the girl *in the red dress*.

Some nouns and the prepositions they are usually used with:

to	for	on	with	various
access	admiration	attack	collision	crime against
addiction	appetite	ban	contrast	grudge against
allergy	bid	claim	correspondence	anger at
answer	cure	comment	date	bond between
damage	demand	crackdown	dealings	escape from
introduction	dislike	effect	dissatisfaction	excerpt from
reply	love	hold	familiarity	freedom from
return	need	insistence	link	awareness of
solution	respect	reflection	quarrel	authority over
threat	search	tax	relationship	control over

TASK 1:

Write some sentences with prepositional phrases using the nouns in the above table, e.g. *I have great admiration for the musicals of Boulbil and Schonberg.*

'To' clauses (non-finite clauses)

For example: Even in this modern age, we still need people *to work in factories*.

Some nouns which usually have a 'to' clause after them:

ability	desire	readiness	urge
attempt	failure	reason	way
chance	need	refusal	willingness

TASK 2:

Write some sentences with 'to' clauses using the nouns in the above table, e.g. *I feel a compulsion to watch television.*

Appositional phrases

For example, Cinderella, *the ragged kitchen maid*, also wanted to go to the ball.

TASK 3:

Using the example above, write some more sentences containing appositional phrases.

49. Themes

NOTE: the term 'theme' refers to the ideas expressed in a poem (or other text).

ANALYSIS OF THEMES

Trace the development of the poet's ideas in detail throughout the poem. Note particularly any new ideas, contrasts or developments. Give evidence from the text(s).

POETIC TECHNIQUES

Refer to any poetic techniques which are important in presenting the theme, e.g. where a poet uses ambiguity to make the reader think about an issue. Give evidence from the text(s).

PERSONAL RESPONSE

Give your own response to the ideas expressed by the poet, e.g. do you agree with the ideas? Give an evaluation of the poem, saying what you liked and disliked, what worked well, and what was less effective.

50. *Toads*

Toads

Why should I let the toad *work*
  Squat on my life?
Can't I use my wit as a pitchfork
  And drive the brute off?

Six days of the week it soils
  With its sickening poison –
Just for paying a few bills!
  That's out of proportion.

Lots of folk live on their wits:
  Lecturers, lispers,
Losels, lobtolly-men, louts –
  They don't end as paupers:

Lots of folk live up lanes
  With fires in a bucket,
Eat windfalls and tinned sardines –
  They seem to like it.

Their nippers have got bare feet,
  Their unspeakable wives
Are skinny as whippets – and yet
  No one actually *starves*.

Ah, were I courageous enough
  To shout *Stuff your pension!*
But I know, all too well, that's the stuff
  That dreams are made on:

For something sufficiently toad-like
  Squats in me, too:
Its hunkers are heavy as hard luck,
  And cold as snow.

And will never allow me to blarney
  My way to getting
The fame and the girl and the money
  All at one sitting.

I don't say, one bodies the other
  One's spiritual truth;
But I do say it's hard to lose either.
  When you have both.

Philip Larkin

DISCUSSION:

- Generally, what is Larkin saying about work?
- How does he develop his ideas about work, verse by verse?
- What poetic techniques give force to his ideas?
- Why can he not act on his opinions in real life?
- What is he saying in the last verse?

51. *Follower*

Follower

My father worked with a horse-plough,
His shoulders globed like a full sail strung
Between the shafts and the furrow.
The horses strained at his clicking tongue.

An expert. He would set the wing
And fit the bright steel-pointed sock.
The sod rolled over without breaking.
At the headrig, with a single pluck

Of reins, the sweating team turned round
And back into the land. His eye
Narrowed and angled at the ground,
Mapping the furrow exactly.

I stumbled in his hob-nailed wake,
Fell sometimes on the polished sod;
Sometimes he rode me on his back
Dipping and rising to his plod.

I wanted to grow up and plough,
To close one eye, stiffen my arm.
All I ever did was follow
In his broad shadow round the farm.

I was a nuisance, tripping, falling,
Yapping always. But today
It is my father who keeps stumbling
Behind me, and will not go away.

Seamus Heaney

DISCUSSION:

● What can you learn about the old methods of ploughing from the poem?

● How can you tell from the poet's diction that he has first-hand knowledge of ploughing?

● Pick out examples of poetic language which bring the description of ploughing to life?

● What can we deduce from verse 5 about how successful Heaney was at ploughing?

● Try to explain the sudden shift in perspective in the last two and a half lines of verse 6.

Experiments

Unit 5: Lesson 4

70 minutes approx.

Objectives

Word: Wd7 recognise layers of meaning in the writer's choice of words, e.g. *connotation*.

Reading: Rd16 analyse ways in which different cultural contexts and traditions have influenced language and style, e.g. *black British poetry*.

Writing: Wr17 cite specific and relevant textual evidence to justify critical judgements about texts.

Speaking and Listening: S&L9 discuss and evaluate conflicting evidence to arrive at a considered viewpoint.

Word/Sentence Activity:

Teach the term *connotations* using resource 52, Connotations.

Introduction:

Explain to students that poetry is at the 'cutting edge' of language. Modern poets are highly experimental. There are no rules in poetry, and anything is possible. This lesson will focus on two examples.

Shared reading of The Future and 10 V. Trendy Things to do 1960s Style (resources 53 and 54).

Development:

Students, in groups of 3–4, discuss the questions following each poem.

The next step is for students to write their own experimental poem. They are free to write anything, but a good way to start is to use one of the poems as a model. Suggestions for writing are given after each poem.

Plenary:

Share work done so far.

Homework:

Write a final version of the experimental poem.

Follow-up:

Get your students to experiment with poetry-writing computer programs, several of which are available on the internet. For example see:

http://www.webcom.com/wordings/artofwrite/poetrygenerator.html
http://www.op.net/~moonloon/Home/poem.html
http://www.literacyonline.com

My favourite is: http://cpcug.org/user/jelks/poetry/js/

Most of these ask for user input, e.g. 'Write a noun', 'Write an adjective to describe your noun', etc. They then mix up your input in interesting and unexpected ways to produce poems – some of them even rhyme!

Though such mechanical processes can never produce good poetry, they can help students in two ways:

◉ They can help them to understand what poetry is, i.e. it is NOT prose, set out in lines which sometimes end with rhyme and decorated with a few similes and metaphors, it is a different, more telegraphic way of saying things.

◉ It can give them the rough draft of a poem which they can develop into something worthwhile.

52. Connotations

Words, in addition to their literal meanings (which are called *denotative meanings* by linguists) often have implied meanings known as *connotations*.

Some writers, particularly advertisers and poets, manipulate the connotations of words to powerful effect. For example, note how connotations have been used to reinforce the basic message of this advertisement:

USE **LARCH** BATHROOM CLEANSER

Fresh as a pine forest

Kills every germ known to science

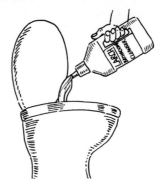

NOTES:

- The product is called *Larch* because its connotations are fresh-smelling trees, not foul-smelling toilets (*pine forest* is used for the same reasons later on).

- *Bathroom* is used because its connotations are *cleanness, bathing, washing*, etc. The illustration shows that the main use of the product is to clean toilets, but toilets are dirty, smelly things which the advertiser does not wish to associate too closely with the product. It is interesting to note the increasing use of this euphemism. Next time you go to buy *toilet tissue*, look how many brands now label it *bathroom tissue*. Of course, the manufacturers have done this to avoid the negative connotations of *toilet*.

- *Cleanse* is frequently used by advertisers instead of *clean* because it carries the connotations of a gentler, more wholesome process.

- *Fresh* – a word often used by advertisers. Its connotations are something straight from nature – yet the product is basically a mixture of processed chemicals.

- *Science* – the connotation is of a complex formula developed in a laboratory. The product is actually a mixture of simple chemicals disguised with a pine aroma.

- The overall effect of these connotations is to make the reader believe that by cleaning their toilet with LARCH they will achieve the freshness of nature with a scientifically-designed formula.

TASK

Find an advertisement on a product in your house, e.g. cereal packet, conditioner, magazine and note how the writer has used the connotations of words.

53. *The Future*

The future

The Future does not look like this . . .

you are
here

PAST _____ FUTURE _____ END
 PRESENT

The Future looks more like this . . .

or this . . .

or this . . . you
are
here

Roger McGough

NOTE:

This is a 'diagram poem'. In other words it combines diagrams with words to try to express an idea.

WRITING:

Try to write your own 'diagram poem' or 'doodle poem' in which you use words with diagrams or doodles to express an idea. If you are stuck for an idea, write about one of the themes of the poems studied so far: *war, city life* or *work*.

54. 10 V. Trendy Things to do 1960s Style

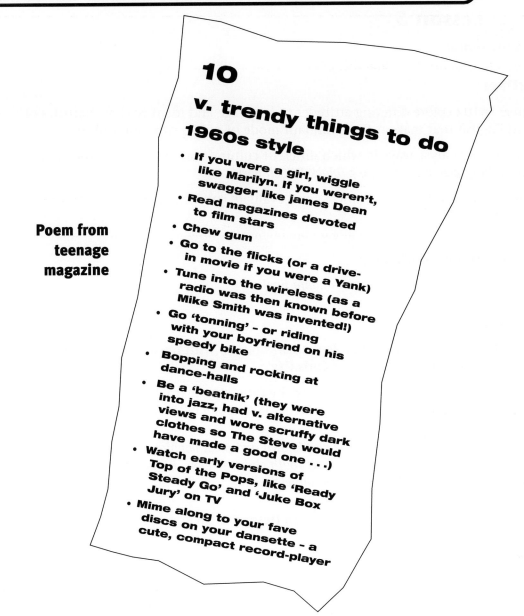

Poem from teenage magazine

10

v. trendy things to do 1960s style

- If you were a girl, wiggle like Marilyn. If you weren't, swagger like james Dean
- Read magazines devoted to film stars
- Chew gum
- Go to the flicks (or a drive-in movie if you were a Yank)
- Tune into the wireless (as a radio was then known before Mike Smith was invented!)
- Go 'tonning' – or riding with your boyfriend on his speedy bike
- Bopping and rocking at dance-halls
- Be a 'beatnik' (they were into jazz, had v. alternative views and wore scruffy dark clothes so The Steve would have made a good one . . .)
- Watch early versions of Top of the Pops, like 'Ready Steady Go' and 'Juke Box Jury' on TV
- Mime along to your fave discs on your dansette – a cute, compact record-player

NOTE:

This is a 'found poem'. The author saw the text in a teenage article in *Jackie* magazine, recognised its potential, and with a few changes to wording and setting out, presented it as a poem.

DISCUSSION:

How do the connotations of some of the words and phrases help to evoke the 1960s?

WRITING:

Either:

Adapt the above poem to the 1950s, 1970s, 1980s or 1990s (you will need to do some research to make it convincing – ask your parents or grandparents).

Or:

Write/discover your own 'found poem' in which you adapt some interesting text from a magazine/newspaper/cereal packet, etc. If you are stuck for an idea, write about one of the themes in the poems studied so far: *war, city life* or *work*.

Benjamin Zephaniah

Unit 5: Lesson 5

70 minutes approx.

Objectives

Sentence: Sn10 explore differing attitudes to language and identify characteristics of standard English that make it the dominant mode of public communication.

Reading: Rd16 analyse ways in which different cultural contexts and traditions have influenced language and style, e.g. *black British poetry*.

Speaking and Listening: S&L9 discuss and evaluate conflicting evidence to arrive at a considered viewpoint.

Word/Sentence Activity:

Using resource 55, revise the term *standard English*.

Introduction:

Note: if possible, try to get hold of Zephaniah's poetry with music. The titles of the albums are 'Rasta' and 'Big Boys Don't Make Girls Cry'.

Introduce Benjamin Zephaniah by reading the following text which is the introduction to *The Dread Affair*, Benjamin Zephaniah, Arena, ISBN 009939250X.

> *Benjamin Zephaniah is probably the best known and most popular of Britain's younger performing poets. He appears regularly at youth clubs, schools, hospitals, and book shops, as well as at more commercial venues and on television.*

Shared reading of *I meditate* and *News at Ten* (resources 56 and 57).

Development:

Ask students to reread each poem and do the tasks after each one (see resources 56 and 57).

Plenary:

Go over the questions and tasks on resources 56 and 57, *I meditate* and *News at Ten*.

Homework:

Based on work done in this lesson, write an account of standard English and compare it with the English used by Zephaniah.

Follow-up:

Explore Black English as used in hip-hop and rap.

55. Standard English

Standard English is the form of the English language that has been standardised over the centuries and which is catalogued in dictionaries and grammar books. Important dates in the standardisation of English are:

1066 – the old standard English (the West Saxon dialect of Anglo-Saxon) was displaced among the ruling class by the Norman French spoken by William and his followers.

1362 – English became the 'official' language of England once again, replacing Norman French after 296 years. In this year it was decreed that English should be used for the proceedings of parliament and as a language of record in the law courts.

1476 – Caxton set up the first printing press in the precincts of Westminster Abbey. His publications had the effect of standardising the grammar, vocabulary and spelling on the dialect of English used in the south-east of England.

1755 – *'Dictionary of the English Language'* was published by Samuel Johnson. The first true dictionary, this remarkable work contains over 40,000 entries. It was highly influential in further standardising meaning, spelling and pronunciation.

1828 – *'An American Dictionary of the English Language'*, by Noah Webster, laid down the standard for American English by cataloguing the differences between British English and American English. It also included an attempt at spelling reform based on simplifying certain spellings, e.g. *catalog, center, tire,* etc.

Twentieth century – science, industry, pop music, air travel and the internet take the two standards of English (British and American) worldwide.

DISCUSSION:

- Give examples of non-standard English, e.g. dialect forms.

- Give examples of other differences between British English and American English.

- Why do you think the above events were so influential in standardising the language?

- Why is it important that every student should have a good command of standard English?

- What is the value of non-standard forms of English?

56. *I Meditate*

I Meditate

I meditate over the paper and pen
and words gather in my head,
and from this point there is no stopping I
for words get heavy like lead
I let them go into rhythms
that hop to my satisfaction
to scribe I aim don't seek no fame
for that is just distraction.
I shall scribe to my ghost
'cause the shores of life's coast
to I is vank illusion
let the pen run away
'cause the words of today
must deal with this oppression
take me here take me there cause I don't care
my head is always willing
I recite in my sleep I don't need to count sheep
and this is just the beginning

Benjamin Zephaniah

DISCUSSION:

- In this poem, Zephaniah describes his creative process. Explain it in your own words.

- What poetic techniques does Zephaniah use to describe his creative process?

- Which words and phrases suggest his interest in music, rap and performance poetry?

- What are his reasons for writing?

57. News at Ten

News at Ten

Dis is the 'News at Ten'
there is a riot in Miami again
dis is the 'News at Ten'
there is a war in Miami again
riot in sight, a riotous sound
a bullet in de head, black youth drops down
run go tell your friend, about dis report from the 'News at Ten'
I heard it on the 'News at One'
they don't know how it begun
I heard it on a newsflash
it's a holiday city, but youths have no cash
it seems they have good weather reports, and they have
    multiracial sports
Trevor McDonald is Lenny Henry*
both have no voice to represent me
check dis Zephaniah news, as you celebrate, I bring the blues
reminding all my so-called friends, there is a riot in Miami again.

Benjamin Zephaniah

*Trevor MacDonald is a black newsreader, Lenny Henry is a black comedian.

DISCUSSION:

- Why does Zephaniah say 'both have no voice to represent me'? Why does he think this even though both are black?

- How does the 'Zephaniah news' differ from the 'official' news?

GENERAL

Investigate how Zephaniah represents Black English in his poetry by drawing up a chart like the following:

BLACK ENGLISH	STANDARD ENGLISH
. . . no stopping I.	. . . no stopping me.

Issues

Unit 5: Lesson 6

70 minutes approx.

Objectives

Sentence: Sn10 explore differing attitudes to language and identify characteristics of standard English that make it the dominant mode of public communication.

Reading: Rd16 analyse ways in which different cultural contexts and traditions have influenced language and style.

Writing: Wr13 present a case persuasively enough to gain the attention and influence the responses of a specified group of readers.

Starter Activity:

Revise how to analyse the rhythm pattern of a poem:

* Read a few lines aloud with a strong emphasis.

* Mark in the stressed syllables with an accent mark /.

For example:

```
  /          /         /             /
I meditate over the paper and pen
        /     /    /        /
and words gather in my head . . .
```

Introduction:

Shared reading of *Superstar on Guitar* and *Modern Slavery* (resources 58 and 59).

Development:

Ask students to reread the poems and do the tasks following each one (see resources 58 and 59).

Plenary:

Discuss the tasks on the resource sheets.

Homework:

Ask students to complete the written task on resource 59, *Modern Slavery*.

Follow-up:

Investigate the songs of Bob Marley. His songs are more than just pop songs as they contain some impassioned personal expression and political commentary.

58. *Superstar on guitar*

Superstar on guitar

Hail, Prince Leroy, how are you?
I don't see you for a year or two,
cool said Leroy cool I say
then Prince Leroy went away.
Hail Prince Leroy come back here
we use to run wild out there
in the blues dance in the ghetto
don't tell me that you forget now.

Leroy move forward to I
Leroy have on shirt and tie.
Leroy looking very slick
he now walk with walking stick.
Leroy said say who you are
I can say I am superstar
I found fame with my guitar
go and ask my manager.

I said Leroy this don't matter
we can still be cool together,
we can still sing songs of praise
Leroy looked slightly amazed.
I said Leroy think again
don't let money buy your brain
don't let stardom buy you out
Leroy man don't mek me shout.

Leroy stood next to a wall
this is how the mighty fall,
Leroy said I now live good
I have a house of brick and a cottage of wood,
I have a real fast car and a real slick chick
I can earn my money quick,
I take 'coke' and go to Mars
I have gold like chocolate bars.

Check this all you Leroys now
he who rise must fall somehow,
nice of you to play guitar
but why should you turn superstar.
Hope your guilt now burns inside
have you lost your ghetto pride,
Leroy now is superstar
one time Leroy was my spa.

Benjamin Zephaniah

DISCUSSION:

- Analyse the rhythm pattern of the poem.

- Analyse the rhyme scheme.

- Highlight all words and phrases that are written in 'Black English'

- How has fame changed Leroy?

- What is Zephaniah's opinion of Leroy and people like him?

59. *Modern slavery*

Modern slavery

Who says where who say when
who says stop to start again
who dictates where to go
moves you round to and fro,
you might work ina factory
de unemployed will never free
de situation look to me just like slavery,
modern slavery it mek you militant
modern slavery it mek you rave and rant
modern slavery you do not need tuition
to learn dat dis slave driving is done by television,
fight it bravely, modern slavery.

Every time you sign at the dole office
dem tax us and tek de money pay fe rockets
we pay fe wars their civilization is high
some house have fifty bedrooms
some house is like pig sty,
and they have many millions and they give us
a share, health workers will riot to keep welfare,
and in high court de circle is complete,
de judge is a rapist and de jury is asleep,
you want to shout for justice but you cannot advertise,
starving faces on a poster don't make you any wise
to cover up hypocrisy they setting up a charity
they'll make a documentary, modern slavery,
slavery here we go again modern slavery
I want to see an end to modern slavery
hear it ever time, sellout on de radio, check it out
here we go slavery, fight it fight it bravely.

Well if you try to fight it like Nicaragua dem say
you have a contact in Russia.
American have contact wid de Mafia but dem kill you
if you talk wid Cuba, see,
freedom of speech is a burning illusion and as
you work you die from pollution,
what I want see is a free Chile, until den I fight bravely.

Who says where who says when
who says stop to start again
who dictates where to go
moves you around to and fro,
some might slave in a factory
de unemployed are never free
dis is de documentary called
modern slavery.

Benjamin Zephaniah

DISCUSSION:

- What does Zephaniah mean by 'modern slavery'?

- What examples of injustice does he give?

- How do television, radio, the law, the taxation system, the benefit system and international politics contribute to 'modern slavery' in the poet's opinion?

- Do you agree with the opinions expressed in this poem?

WRITING

Zephaniah's poem is an impassioned attack on the *status quo* (Latin for 'the way things are'). EITHER – rewrite and develop his arguments in the form of a serious newspaper article; OR write a serious newspaper article to refute (argue against) his arguments.

Black English

Unit 5: Lesson 7

70 minutes approx.

Word/Sentence Activity:

The exploration of Black English in this lesson is an excellent opportunity to learn about a wide range of language concepts. As a basis for the lesson, students will need to understand the following terms. Some of them, such as accent and dialect, can be revised quickly, others will need fuller discussion.

Accent – different pronunciation of Standard English, e.g. most speakers in the south would say 'ba:th' (long a); whereas most speakers in the north would say 'bath' (short a).

Black English – a variety or dialect of English. There are many different varieties of Black English ranging from Jamaican Black English, American Ebonics, Black Estuary English (as spoken by Ali G.) and a wide range of creoles.

Creole – a variety of English which has been strongly influenced by a local language, e.g. Hausa. These can be very different from standard English.

Dialect – a variety of standard English with differences of grammar, vocabulary and pronunciation.

Ebonics – an academic term for Black English (coined in 1973 in St Louis, Missouri).

Language – this has been defined as 'a dialect with an army and a navy'. Some languages are so similar (e.g. the Scandinavian languages) that they would be described as dialects if they existed within the same political boundaries.

Language variety – a broader term for dialect which avoids the negative connotations (i.e. that it is inferior) that word has acquired.

Introduction:

Shared reading of resource 60, 'Black English' Proposal Draws Fire.

Development:

Students discuss the questions at the end of resource 60, 'Black English' Proposal Draws Fire.

The next step is for them to write a description of Black English, using their notes from Lessons 1 and 2, and any other information they can find in the article.

Homework:

Ask students to do more research into Black English, e.g. by visiting http://www.africana.com/tt_262.htm, and then to write a final draft of their description of Black English.

Follow-up:

Investigate poetry written in another variety of English, e.g. Scots dialect, Yorkshire dialect, Cockney, etc.

60. 'Black English' Proposal Draws Fire

'Black English' proposal draws fire

Symbolic move in Oakland touches a nerve

December 22, 1996

(CNN) – So far it's little more than a vague idea, but a proposal by a California school board last week to recognize Black English as a second language has already sparked a firestorm of debate.

'I am incensed,' said poet *Maya Angelou*, who recited one of her poems at President Clinton's inauguration. 'The very idea that African-American language is a language separate and apart can be very threatening, because it can encourage young men and women not to learn standard English.'

The Rev. Jesse Jackson also blasted the proposal, which was announced Wednesday by the California School Board to officially recognize Black English, also known as Ebonics, a term combining 'ebony' and 'phonics.'

'While we are fighting in California trying to extend affirmative action and fighting to teach our children so they become more qualified for jobs, in Oakland some madness has erupted over making slang talk a second language,' Jackson said in a statement.

'You don't have to go to school to learn to talk garbage,' he said.

School board members said the idea behind the proposal is to improve performance of black students, who make up 53 percent of the district and 71 percent of those enrolled in special-education courses.

'What we are doing in Oakland is providing our teachers and parents with the tools to address the diverse languages our children bring into the classroom,' said a school board statement.

'We have to acknowledge that all of our students do not come to us speaking standard English,' added Lucella Harrison, president of the Oakland School Board.

How the new policy will be implemented isn't yet clear, but Oakland school officials have said they may ask for federal money to help African-American students who primarily speak Ebonics.

Black English speaking students may be placed in classes that will help them to learn standard English, and teachers may be trained to understand Black English.

Oakland's decision directly affects only the 52,000 students in the district. But the idea that Black English is a 'genetically-based' language with roots in Western Africa – and not just slang – is highly symbolic of the nation's larger racial divide.

Many believe Oakland's move has widespread implications on race, language and society. 'This hurts the kids, that's the real tragedy of it,' said John Fonte, a visiting scholar in education at the American Enterprise Institute in Washington. 'The way to learn English is to study English.'

Black English has already been taught in a number of schools such as Ann Arbor, Michigan. But Oakland appears to be the first district to make a system-wide change.

The American Speech, Language and Hearing Association has classified Black English as a social dialect.

English words in Black English tend to lose a 'd' following a vowel, so 'good' becomes 'goo,' and the final 'th' is sometime is replaced with 'f', so 'with' becomes 'wif.'

Critics say encouraging this non-standard English could give students the idea that Ebonics is a viable language in the workplace, a mistake that could hinder their job searches and careers.

Said Ryan Cameron, a rap radio disc jockey: 'It's something that people use among their friends, but it's not something that they have to do to get ahead or have to do to get a job.'

CNN News

DISCUSSION:

- The issue discussed in this article could apply to any dialect of English. Make a list of the dialects you know. Then rank them in order of similarity to standard English (those that only differ slightly at the top, those that differ a great deal at the bottom).

- Do you think that teaching students in their own dialect (whether Black English, Scots, Cockney or any other) would 'improve performance'?

- What does the writer of the article think are the biggest disadvantages of teaching Ebonics (Black English)?

WRITING:

Write a description of Black English, using your notes from previous lessons, and any other information you can find in the article.

Writing About a Poet

Unit 5: Lesson 8

70 minutes approx.

Objectives

Word: Wd6 know and use the terms that are useful for analysing language, e.g. *conjunctions.*

Reading: Rd16 analyse ways in which different cultural contexts and traditions have influenced language and style, e.g. *black British poetry.*

Writing: Wr17 cite specific and relevant textual evidence to justify critical judgements about texts.

Starter Activity:

Revise and extend knowledge of conjunctions using resource 61.

Introduction:

Review all the resources used in this unit, and read one more poem by Benjamin Zephaniah: 'Pen Rhythm' (resource 62).

Discuss the questions at the end of the poem.

Development:

Give out resource 63, Template for Writing About a Poet, and explain how to use it.

- Encourage students to support key points with quotations from the poems. These should be short, i.e. not more than two lines – short phrases are often enough to exemplify a point.

- Explain the two different methods of organising material in sections 1 and 2.

Method 1 (easiest)

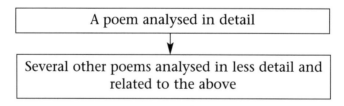

Method 2 (harder)

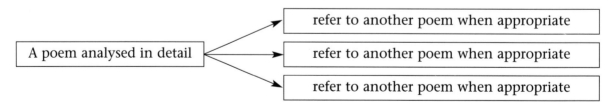

- In the section on style, students should explain about Black English and how Zephaniah uses it. They should also compare the patterns of rhythm and rhyme with those used in rap.

Plenary:

Review progress on the essay on Benjamin Zephaniah's poetry.

Homework:

Finish the essay on Benjamin Zephaniah's poetry. Encourage students to use conjunctions (see resource 61) and connectives (see resource 31) to enable them to express their ideas in a sophisticated way.

Follow-up:

Read more of Benjamin Zephaniah's work in

The Dread Affair: Collected Poems, Benjamin Zephaniah, Arena, ISBN 009939250X

61. Conjunctions

Conjunctions join clauses together. There are two types of conjunctions, *coordinating conjunctions* and *subordinating conjunctions*.

Coordinating conjunctions join statements with equal weight into *compound sentences*. The coordinating conjunctions are: *and, but, or.*

Subordinating conjunctions are used to add a *subordinate clause* (usually an *adverbial clause*, i.e. a clause which acts like an *adverb*). This results in a *complex sentence.*

The following table shows the different types of adverbial clauses and the conjunctions used with them:

TYPE OF ADVERBIAL CLAUSE	CONJUNCTIONS USED WITH CLAUSE
CONCESSION	although, though, while
CONDITIONAL	if, unless
MANNER	as, like
PLACE	where, wherever
PURPOSE	in order to, so, that
REASON	as, because, since
RESULT	so that
TIME	after, as, until, before, since, when, while

You can see from this table that conjunctions enable us to develop and modify ideas in sophisticated ways. They are therefore particularly useful in argumentative or discursive writing and writing literary essays.

TASK:

Experiment with conjunctions by playing the following game:

- Make a set of Conjunction Cards based on the list above (26 in total).

- Your partner makes a statement about an issue, e.g. 'Global warming will get worse'.

- You give him a Conjunction Card selected at random and he/she has to use it to develop his/her statement, e.g. '*unless* we reduce the output of greenhouse gases', or, '*although* some believe that global warming is a modern myth.'

- NOTE: if the conjunction will not fit the statement, try another. If that will not fit, ask your partner to rephrase the statement.

62. *Pen Rhythm*

Pen rhythm

No silver or gold I have no riches
I have no castle on high,
certain things a one can have
and no money can buy,
check aspects of city life
check the earthman brain,
still cool and easy bring it down
pen rhythm take the strain.
The rhythm of the pen goes bubbling
dancing round the page
no decease can't cripple it
can't dead of old age,
the rhythm of the pen goes too and fro
high and low where you can't go
the rhythm of the pen will not stop now
pen rhythm is in full rage.

People always talking
tales of this and that,
society keeps on sucking like a drunk vampire bat,
fighters keep on fighting the ideas that take control
ideas that rap and trap some boys and take away their soul,
baldhead boys are running
first place in rat race,
there once was a barber here
but that barber got chased,
pharaoh's girls keep coming
they shall find their place
what they cannot see on Earth they try to see in space.

The rhythm of the pen goes ring ding dong
left and right and can't go wrong
the pen plans the rhythm and the rhythm sings a song
the strain is on the rhythm but the rhythm well strong,
the rhythm of the pen goes here and there
always with harmony always with care
the rhythm is full still there is some spare
pen rhythm get wild pen rhythm don't fear.

Benjamin Zephaniah

DISCUSSION:

* What does Zephaniah believe to be the value of poetry?

* Give some examples of striking metaphors and similes and say how they work.

* What do you think he is trying to say in the section beginning 'baldhead boys . . .'?

63. Template for Writing About a Poet

1. INTRODUCTION: Give brief background details.

2. ONE POEM IN DETAIL: Choose the poem which includes the best examples of the poet's themes and style and analyse it in detail. Give evidence from the text.

3. OTHER POEMS: Write more briefly about several other poems, relating them to the poem in section 2. (Note: these two sections can be integrated by referring to other poems as you write section 2.) Give evidence from the texts.

4. MAIN THEMES: Identify the poet's main themes and discuss them. Use resource 49, 'Themes' to help you. Give evidence from the text(s).

5. STYLE: Describe the poet's style. This can be done by explaining how he or she uses the poetic techniques described on resource 45, Poetic Techniques. Give evidence from the text(s).

6. CONCLUSION: Give a personal response, i.e. what do you particularly admire/appreciate about this poet's work?

UNIT 6: MODERN DRAMA

Title of unit: MODERN DRAMA	
Resources	
Book: *Spoonface Steinberg*, by Lee Hall, BBC, ISBN 0563 383984	
Cassette: *Spoonface Steinberg*, ZBBC 2058, ISBN 0563 382465	

Year: 9	Term: 3, second half	Duration: lessons 6/8	Set: All

NLS objectives		NC objectives
I Luv You Jimmy Spud	Sn10, S&L11, S&L15	En 1 3a) make different types of contributions to groups, adapting their speech to their listeners and the activity.
Issues	Wd: various, Sn: various, Wr16, S&L15	
Spoonface Steinberg	S&L11, S&L15	En1 11b) devising, scripting and performing in plays;
The Character of Spoonface	Rd11, Wr9, S&L15	En1 11c) discussing and reviewing their own and others' performances.
Radio Simulation	Wd: various, Sn: various, Rd: various, Wr: various, S&L: various	En 2 8b) recent and contemporary drama.
		En 3 1 writing to imagine, explore, entertain, persuade, argue, advise, analyse, review, comment.
		En 3 2 planning and drafting.

Teaching sequence	Outcomes
Week 1: I luv you Jimmy Spud Issues	Research religious beliefs of Christians and Hindus. *Write a discursive essay on one of the issues raised by the play.
Week 2: Spoonface Steinberg The Character of Spoonface	Research autism. *Character study of Spoonface.
Week 3/4: Radio Simulation	For each student: *Contribution to a group radio soap opera. *1 major and 2 or more minor contributions to the radio channel. A class radio channel.
	Assessment pieces

I Luv You Jimmy Spud

Unit 6: Lesson 1

70 minutes approx.

Objectives

Sentence: Sn10 explore differing attitudes to language and identify characteristics of standard English that make it the dominant mode of public communication – *and compare it with the Geordie dialect.*

Speaking and Listening: S&L11 recognise, evaluate and extend the skills and techniques they have developed through drama; S&L15 write critical evaluations of performances they have seen or in which they have participated, identifying the contributions of the writer, director and actors.

Word/Sentence Activity:

Ask students to investigate the way the Geordie dialect has been used in the play. Begin by explaining that 'Geordie' is a term referring to people from the north-east of England.

One way to investigate the dialect is to draw up a chart in two columns, as follows:

GEORDIE	STANDARD ENGLISH
oot	out
deein'	doing
me	my

The scene 'Home' (pages 13–16) can be investigated for the starter activity. Other dialect terms can be added as the play-reading progresses.

Introduction and development:

Working in groups of 6 (see cast list on page 11), students perform the play reading from the text.

This can be done in the classroom, but will be more effective if it can be done in a space in which students can move around freely such as the hall or a drama studio.

As students read through the play, allocate a different scene to each group. When they have read the whole play, they should polish this particular scene for later performance (see below). When polishing the scene ask students to:

● Speak the lines clearly and naturally. Note that it is not necessary to try to imitate the Geordie accent. The best approach is to speak the lines in the local accent (or in each individual's natural voice) adapting the spellings which are used to show Geordie sounds. The main thing is to bring the script alive.

● Plan basic moves. These will have to be kept simple because there is not time for students to learn parts, so they will always have their scripts in their hands.

● Where facilities allow, plan basic lighting and sound effects.

Plenary:

Evaluate work done so far by inviting each group to comment on how well group members thought they did on each of the three categories listed above, particularly the first.

Homework:

Explain that the lesson following the performance will be used to discuss the ideas and issues raised by the play. It would therefore be valuable to carry out background research in Christian and Hindu (and any other religions) beliefs about God, suffering, angels, life after death, etc.

Follow-up:

In a following lesson, perform the whole play, with each group performing its allotted scene.

Some students may be interested in further pursuing the investigation of the Geordie dialect. They can have fun experimenting with the 'English to Geordie Translator' at http://www.geordie.org.uk/ The site also contains links to more serious information about Geordie dialect and culture. This is the introduction to the site:

Alreet lads an lasses. Welcome to The English to Geordie translator. But what's a Geordie you may be asking yourself, the site *Geordie Passions* is a scrap book of Geordie culture which will help explain more, but in essence its them canny fowk from the North East of England sometimes wrongly but understandably mistaken for Scots or Irish to the unaquainted.

Issues

Unit 6: Lesson 2

70 minutes approx.

Objectives

Word: various.

Sentence: various.

Writing: Wr16 present a balanced analysis of a situation, text, issue or set of ideas, taking into account a range of evidence and opinions.

Speaking and Listening: S&L15 write critical evaluations of performances they have seen or in which they have participated, identifying the contributions of the writer, director and actors.

Starter Activity:

Give students a 'discursive writing kit' consisting of the following:
Resource 30, Pronouns (see Unit 4, Lesson 3)
Resource 31, Connectives (see Unit 4, Lesson 4)
Resource 48, Qualifiers (see Unit 5, Lesson 3)
Resource 61, Conjunctions (see Unit 5, Lesson 8)
Resource 65, Discursive Essay Template (see Unit 6: Lesson 2)

Students should spend ten minutes in small groups, pairs or individually revising the above skills according to their needs.

Introduction

Remind students of the content of the play. A good way to do this is to re-read pp. 24–6, 'Does God Exist?' and briefly discuss what went before and what comes after.

Development

Working in groups of 3–4 students discuss the ideas in the play.

The next step is to write one or both of the summaries under the heading 'Writing'. Note that these are similar to the summaries required on many GCSE papers in which information on a particular topic or theme has to be retrieved from a text and represented in the candidate's own words. No word limit is set for this exercise. A good summary is one which includes all the relevant information expressed in coherent standard English.

Plenary:

Go over the discussion questions on resource 64. Notes: generally, most religions believe that suffering is not caused by God but by evil and/or man's free will. Some religions see suffering as the means through which we learn and grow spiritually – which is what happens to Jimmy Spud in the play.

All religions claim that they are the true religion. We can only know God through symbols, and symbols are culturally specific, so perhaps all established religions are just ways of trying to understand that which is impossible to understand.

The basic situation of the play is hilarious – a not very bright Geordie boy becoming an angel. We laugh at his early attempts at understanding and behaving like an angel, but Jimmy grows throughout the play, and the reader begins to take him more seriously until at the end his transfiguration is quite believable. There are many other examples of humour.

Homework:

Ask students to write a discursive essay examining one of the issues raised by the play, e.g. 'Does God Exist?' Encourage them to make full use of the support provided by 'The discursive writing kit' (see starter activity above).

Follow-up:

Share with students the classic arguments for the existence of God ...

64. I Luv You Jimmy Spud Questions

DISCUSSION:

- Granddad says, 'Well, if there was a God why would there be war and disease and kids starving in Biafra and all that? (p. 25)

  Why does he think that, war, disease and starvation are evidence that God does not exist? What is your opinion?

- Jimmy says, 'Ragie Patel sez that in Pakistan there's millions iv Gods. And they have different arms and all sorts.' (p. 26).

  If there are many Gods and many religions, how do we know which one is the real God or the true religion?

- Dad says, 'If there is a bliddy God, what's he deing giving me cancer?' (p. 26)

  Do you think this is a good reason not to believe in God? How do you think a Christian priest would answer him? Would the answer given by a Hindu, Muslim, Jew, or believer in any other faith be different?

- The play deals with serious issues including religion, suffering and death. Give some examples of how Lee Hall uses humour to prevent the play from becoming too gloomy.

- What does Dad think is going on when he catches Jimmy with Scout dressed up in his Angel's tunic – which he thinks is a frock? (p. 34) Even though he is wrong about Jimmy, there is a moral here. What is it?

- Jimmy says, 'But Mam, there is no death really' (p. 40)

  What does this show about Jimmy's development as an angel? Do you agree with the statement?

WRITING:

Granddad says, 'Individual salvation's just bourgeois sophistry, son.' (p. 48) Trace other statements by Granddad and write a paragraph summarising his political views.

Re-read 'The Transfiguration of Jimmy Spud' (p. 51) Write a summary of Jimmy Spud's development as an angel.

DISCURSIVE ESSAY:

Write an essay in which you express your opinion about one of the issues raised in the play.

65. Discursive Essay Template

Refer to the following resource sheets to help you with appropriate vocabulary and grammar to marshal your arguments:

- Resource 30, Pronouns
- Resource 31, Connectives
- Resource 48, Qualifiers
- Resource 61, Conjunctions

NOTE: the essay should be a series of paragraphs without subheadings. All the text in the boxes below is for guidance only.

INTRODUCTION
A paragraph introducing the topic you are going to discuss and defining any difficult terms.

BACKGROUND INFORMATION
One or two paragarphs of necessary background information, e.g. in a discussion of religion, some key facts about the beliefs of the main world religions.

ONE SIDE OF THE ARGUMENT
A series of paragraphs, each of which introduces and develops a point in support of one side of the argument.

THE OTHER SIDE OF THE ARGUMENT
A series of paragraphs which explore the other side (or sides) of the argument.

DISCUSSION AND EVALUATION
A series of paragraphs which discuss and evaluate the points made in the two previous sections.

CONCLUSION
A statement of the conclusion arising from the above discussion with one or two of the main reasons for arriving at that conclusion.

Spoonface Steinberg

Unit 6: Lesson 3

70 minutes approx.

Word/Sentence Activity:

Teach the term 'monologue'. A monologue is a drama in which only one person speaks. Discuss the difficulties of:

a) writing an effective monologue; and

b) performing and presenting a monologue.

Introduction:

Listen to the tape of *Spoonface Steinberg*, or read the play in small groups of 3–4 taking sections in turn. Note: the tape takes 60 mins. so, along with the starter activity, it will take up all the lesson time. Development and Plenary will be part of the following lesson.

Homework:

● Re-read the monologue at home.

AND/OR

● Background research into autism.

OR see 'Follow-up'

Follow-up:

Students could create a suffering character and write that character's monologue.

The Character of Spoonface

Unit 6: Lesson 4

70 minutes approx.

Objectives

Word: (not listed) appreciate specific meaning in context of an increasing range of words.

Reading: Rd11 analyse how an author's standpoint can affect meaning in non-literary as well as literary texts.

Writing: Wr9 integrate diverse information into a coherent and comprehensive account.

Speaking and Listening: S&L15 write critical evaluations of performances they have seen or in which they have participated, identifying the contributions of the writer, director and actors.

Word/Sentence Activity:

Define the term: *euphemism.*

Euphemism is the use of roundabout language to replace terms that are considered too blunt or unpleasant. Here are some examples of different types:

- *Passed away, sleeping, rests in peace* are all euphemisms for *dead.*
- *Collateral damage* is an American military euphemism for *casualties of war.*
- *Rodent operative* is a euphemism which attempts to make an unpleasant job (*rat catcher*) sound better.

Introduction:

Briefly recap on the story of Spoonface Steinberg: it is the monologue of a seven-year-old autistic girl dying of cancer in which she shows remarkable insights into her parents' relationship, remarkable number skills, and a moving philosophy of life and death.

Development:

Working in the same small groups, students discuss the questions on resource 66, Spoonface Questions.

The next step is to write one or both of the summaries under the heading 'Writing'. Note that these are similar to the summaries required on many GCSE papers in which information on a particular topic or theme has to be retrieved from a text and represented in the candidate's own words. No word limit is set for this exercise. A good summary is one which includes all the relevant information expressed in coherent standard English.

Plenary:

Go over the discussion questions. Notes: some students may pick up the link between use of the word 'special' in the text and the term 'Special Needs' in school. In the text, Spoonface explores the word 'special'. In schools it describes students who need extra help in one or more subjects. It is a good example of a 'receding euphemism'. Terms to describe students needing extra help slowly pick up negative connotations and have to be replaced. 'Special Needs' replaced 'Remedial'. Ask students to explore the history of words for 'lavatory' for an even better example of this language phenomenon. Students may also like to play the euphemism game at: http://www.westwords.com/GUFFEY/euquiz.html

Amazing skills in autistic patients are well documented, e.g. number skills like Spooface's, artistic skills, etc.

The author makes Spoonface speak in a deliberately ungrammatical way – punctuated by dashes – to represent her autism. However, the content of what she says is often very profound.

The last question is difficult to answer as, like the monologue, its aim is to get the reader/listener to think. Generally, it puts Spoonberg's suffering in context of wider human suffering. This does not lesson our empathy with Spoonface's suffering, but perhaps, by reminding us that suffering is the common lot of humanity, increases our empathy: we may not be autistic, but we may suffer in other ways.

Homework:

Ask students to write the character study outlined on resource 66, Spoonface Questions, for homework.

Follow-up:

Read the other two plays in the collection: *The Love Letters of Ragie Patel* and *The Sorrows of Sandra Saint*.

66. Spoonface Questions

DISCUSSION:

- What is wrong with Spoonface – from birth and later on?

- Why does she prefer 'the proper music' compared to music that other youngsters like?

- How did she come to be called 'Spoonface'?

- What did her dad do that might have made Spoonface worse?

- What is the effect of repeating the word 'special' on p. 142? How is this word used in schools?

- Spoonface, though autistic, has some unusual skills. What are these?

- What is her philosophy of life and her attitude to death?

- How does the way the author makes her speak help the reader/hearer to understand her character?

- How does she react when she hears she is going to die? How do her parents react?

- Other peoples' suffering, e.g. the motorcycle accident, the doctor's description of the concentration camps and Mrs Spud's problems, are referred to in the monologue. How do these affect the way we think about Spoonface's sufferings?

WRITING:

Pick out all the information about her parents' relationship and write a summary of it in your own words.

Pick out all the information about Spoonface's medical condition and write a summary of it in your own words.

SPOONFACE CHARACTER STUDY, OUTLINE:

- Explain Spoonface's medical condition.

- Explain her understanding of the world around her, and her special skills.

- Explain her influence on the people around her, particularly her parents.

- Explain her philosophy of life and her attitude to death.

- Give a personal response to the plight of Spoonface.

Radio Simulation

All lessons

Objectives:

Word: various.

Sentence: various.

Reading: various.

Writing: various.

Speaking and Listening: various.

General:

The aims of this radio simulation are as follows:

- To consolidate writing, speaking and drama skills learned throughout the year.
- To provide a different context for learning in which students have to apply the skills learned in structured literacy lessons in a more open-ended context.
- To use skills resources, writing templates and other supports with greater independence.
- To work collaboratively with clearly defined group and individual goals.

Word/Sentence Activity:

All the skills resources used throughout the year (including resources not in this book) should be made readily available in the classroom, e.g. in a clearly labelled filing cabinet. An index to those resources should be pasted on the front of the cabinet or displayed as a poster.

Students should be encouraged to use these resources to check any word, or sentence-level skills they are not sure about, and to find templates which they may need to support their writing.

Introduction:

The first lesson should begin with some taped examples of a range of radio programmes. Though students may listen to radio, they may be less familiar with radio drama, documentary and discussion programmes.

Organisation:

The organisation is outlined on resource 67, Radio Simulation – Task Sheet. This has been designed to be displayed on a notice board rather than given to each student.

Note that when students are working in pairs or groups, they should ensure that their contribution is identifiable. Where there is doubt, their minor tasks should be individual tasks.

A note on recording:
It is not absolutely necessary to record anything, as most of the valuable work will be done in the process of preparing to record. However, the better the recording (and broadcasting) facility, the higher students' motivation will be. Most schools should be able to provide several cassette recorders (ask colleagues in the Modern Languages and Music departments), many will be able to do better in the form of DAT recorders, mini-disk recorders, and CD-R. The quality of microphones is also important. Try to use good quality microphones on

stands rather than built-in microphones. Perhaps most important of all is to find a number of quiet spaces for recording, as unwanted background noise is one of the easiest ways to spoil a recording.

Each tape (mini-disk or CD) should be clearly labelled with the title of the piece, the names of the participants and the running time. The latter will be important when it comes to putting the final programme together.

The final programme can be put together in a number of ways, depending on the equipment available. If a mixing desk is available (see the Music department), the programme can be put together in a way that is similar to the real thing. A continuity announcer speaks through one channel to announce the next programme, and the tape is played through another channel, having previously been checked through headphones to ensure that the tape is set at the beginning of the programme and that the volume level is correct.

An ordinary cassette recorder with a microphone can be used instead. The tapes can be set up by another student who can use another machine to find the beginning of the appropriate piece.

Development:

Full instructions for students are given on resource 67, Radio Simulation – Task Sheet. Each student is required to do the following tasks:

- Participate in a group Soap Opera scene.
- Participate in ONE major programme (see list on resource 71).
- Participate in at least TWO minor programmes (see list on resource 72).

Within these requirements for outcomes, students should be given complete autonomy over working methods.

Notes on the soap opera:
Students work in groups of 4–5 and follow the instructions on the task sheet. The hardest part is combining the work of different groups into one big soap opera. As one of the aims of this simulation is to encourage independent working, the teacher should keep a light hand on the tiller. By all means give advice, but try to let students sort it out for themselves. If this fails, they can record a series of separate short drama scenes instead.

Plenary:

At the end of each lesson, a short plenary to review progress would be valuable.

Homework:

It would be inappropriate to set specific homework. Students have a series of goals, and they should (for once) be trusted to work towards these goals in their own way, managing their time as they wish.

Follow-up:

The whole experience can be greatly enhanced if the programme is actually broadcast. In a few schools it may be possible to hook up to the tannoy or PA system at break and lunchtimes. However, most schools should be able to arrange for the programme to be broadcast through speakers in the school hall.

67. Radio Simulation – Task Sheet

During this simulation you will be asked to participate in a radio soap opera, ONE major programme and at least TWO minor programmes. You will be working on your own, in pairs or in groups as appropriate (see Task cards for details).

RADIO SOAP

All students should contribute to the radio soap – see resource 68, Task Card – Radio Soap, for details.

MAJOR PROGRAMMES

You should produce one major programme from the list below (further details can be found on resources 71, Task Cards – Major Programmes. You can also put forward your own proposals for programmes to the station manager (your teacher).

- Book review
- Discussion issues
- Documentary
- Film review
- News
- Poetry review

MINOR PROGRAMMES

You should produce at least two minor tasks from the list below (further details can be found on resources 72, Task Cards – Minor Programmes). These can be fitted in at any time.

- Advertisements
- Computer talk
- Ghost story interview
- Quiz show – groups of 4 to 6
- Smash hits!
- Star signs
- Student interviews
- Weather

RECORDING

When you have written, prepared and rehearsed your piece, record it on cassette (or other medium as instructed by the teacher). Label the cassette with the title of the programme and write the exact running time on the label in minutes and seconds. You can record more than one piece on your cassette, but leave a few minutes of blank tape between each item.

68. Task Card – Radio Soap

Work in groups of 4–5. Your task is to write a scene for a radio soap opera.

PART 1

Study the 'Soap Setting' map on resource 69. This is a pictorial map of Seaville – a small seaside town on the south coast of England. It is the setting in which the action of the soap takes place.

Use the character cards from Unit 1. These can be supplemented with the character cards from Unit 4. Each group member now chooses a character from the cards and using the map, decides where the character lives, works, and goes for entertainment.

Practise acting out your character by talking to other characters in your group 'in role'. Ask them, where they went to school, what happened at work, where they are going for their holidays, etc.

The next step is to introduce a situation. This can be done by shuffling the Situation Cards (cut out from resource 70), and choosing a card at random. You should then improvise what happens.

Try this several times, then choose the best of the improvised scenes and develop them. This can be done by structuring the plot more carefully (the plot cards from Unit 1 may help here). Write a first draft of the playscript.

Each group presents its scene to the rest of the class.

PART 2

When all the groups have presented their scenes, look for ways to combine them into one big soap opera. This can be done by:

- Finding a way to bring many of the characters together, e.g. in a pub, a nightclub, a shop, etc.

- Find stories that link together, e.g. a scene about a night out could be linked with another group's scene about 'one too many' by starting with the main characters from both scenes in the same club.

- When writing the final version of the script, interweave the storylines as they do on TV. Thus, five minutes of one story line, could be followed by five minutes of another, followed by another five minutes of the first story line, etc.

PART 3

Redraft the first versions of the scripts into one long soap, divide it up into episodes and act it out onto cassette along with appropriate sound effects.

69. Soap Setting – Seaville

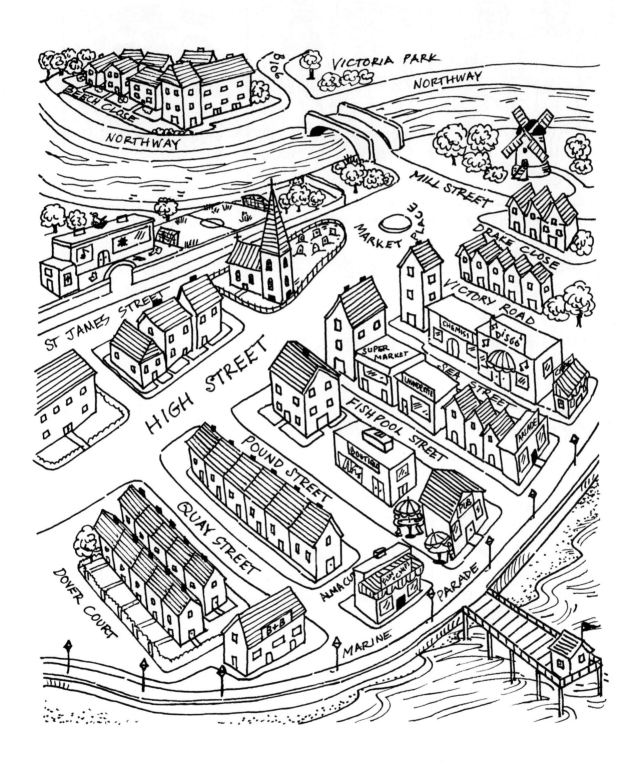

70. Situation Cards

71. Task Cards – Major Programmes

BOOK REVIEW
(Group size: 2–3)

Choose a book to review. This could be one of the books studied this year, e.g. The *Hound of the Baskervilles* or any other book. The programme could include:

* readings from the book
* analysis of character, plot, themes and language
* a discussion forum
* a final rating or recommendation.

DISCUSSION ISSUES
(Group size: 2–6)

Choose an issue to discuss. This could be one of the issues discussed during the year, for example see Units 5 & 6, or any other issue. The programme could be presented as a discussion forum with 3–5 people on the panel or as a debate between two people, or it could be a combination of both. See resource 65, Discursive Essay Template to help the main speakers organise their speeches.

DOCUMENTARY
(Group size: 2–4)

This could be based on one of the many topics covered this year, e.g. about the Sutton Hoo finds. Most of the information could be given by a narrator, but it is important to find ways of breaking this up, e.g.

* interviews with other students acting a part, e.g. of an archaeologist
* visits to locations (use sound effects to give the impression you are there).

FILM REVIEW
(Group size: 2–4)

This could include a review of one of the films seen as part of this year's course of study, or any other film. Use resources 20 and 21, Film Analysis Checklist in Unit 3 to give you ideas about what to include in the programme. Make the programme interesting by including different speakers for different topics. You could extend the programme to include discussion about several recently released films. End with a ratings for each film.

NEWS
(Group size: 2–4)

You could divide this into two parts: national news and school news. Take the national news from daily newspapers, but do not just read out the articles. Pick out the main points and re-tell them in your own words. School news will have to be researched by a team of reporters. The school secretary, heads of year and PE teachers are likely to have interesting information. Try to get a copy of the day's notices. Again, don't just read these things out. Put them in your own words and make them sound interesting.

POETRY REVIEW
(Group size: 2–4)

This programme could include poems by established poets as well as 'new work' by other students. Select a 'Poet of the week' for detailed analysis. This could be one of the poets studied in Unit 5. Use resource 63, Template for Writing About a Poet, in Unit 5 to give you ideas about what to say.

72. Task Cards – Minor Programmes

ADVERTISEMENTS
(Group size: 2–4)
Decide what product you are going to advertise and think up a slogan and a catchy jingle. Ask the Music department for chime bars, glockenspiels, electronic keyboards, etc., so that you can add some musical effects. Close harmony vocals are also effective. Keep it short – 5–10 seconds is about right.

QUIZ SHOW
(Group size: 4–8)
Quiz shows take many forms and there are many examples on radio and television which you could adapt. Make sure the format you choose is suitable for radio and try to give it an educational focus.

SMASH HITS!
(Group size: 1–4)
Individuals could play their favourite records for 10–20 minutes. They should introduce each record in the way that radio DJs do, i.e. with a 'voiceover' the introduction to the record. An alternative is to have a talk show in which the guests express their opinions about the latest records.

STAR SIGNS
(Group size: 1)
This programme consists of horoscope readings for each sign of the zodiac. Reading out all the predictions at once might be boring, so use short 2-minute readings for one sign at a time to break up other programmes.

STUDENT INTERVIEWS
(Group size: 2–8)
There are two ways to do this. Students being interviewed could be themselves, or could pretend to be a famous person. Begin by drawing up a list of useful questions. Try to avoid questions with yes/no answers – the trick is to get the interviewee talking. Ask them about:
- likes and dislikes
- job or school
- hobbies
- current issues.

WEATHER
(Group size: 1)
The best way to do this is to get your data from the Geography department (if they have a weather station) and relate the information to school events, e.g. a cricket match that might be 'rained off'.

GHOST STORY INTERVIEW
(Group size: 2–6)
Interview students about ghosts they have seen, or true ghost stories they have heard. The interviews could be followed by a discussion about whether ghosts exist.

COMPUTER TALK
(Group size: 1–2)
Begin with news about the latest developments in computers and peripherals. Review the latest internet sites and games.